Apress Pocket Guides

Apress Pocket Guides present concise summaries of cutting-edge developments and working practices throughout the tech industry. Shorter in length, books in this series aims to deliver quick-to-read guides that are easy to absorb, perfect for the time-poor professional.

This series covers the full spectrum of topics relevant to the modern industry, from security, AI, machine learning, cloud computing, web development, product design, to programming techniques and business topics too.

Typical topics might include:

- A concise guide to a particular topic, method, function or framework
- Professional best practices and industry trends
- A snapshot of a hot or emerging topic
- Industry case studies
- Concise presentations of core concepts suited for students and those interested in entering the tech industry
- Short reference guides outlining 'need-to-know' concepts and practices.

More information about this series at `https://link.springer.com/bookseries/17385`.

Spec-Driven Development

From Specs to Code with AI Agents

Simon Martinelli

Apress®

Spec-Driven Development: From Specs to Code with AI Agents

Simon Martinelli
Erlach, Switzerland

ISBN-13 (pbk): 979-8-8688-2850-8 ISBN-13 (electronic): 979-8-8688-2851-5
https://doi.org/10.1007/979-8-8688-2851-5

Managing Director, Apress Media LLC: Welmoed Spahr
Acquisitions Editor: Melissa Duffy
Editorial Assistant: Gryffin Winkler

Cover designed by eStudioCalamar

Distributed to the book trade worldwide by Springer Science+Business Media New York, 1 New York Plaza, New York, NY 10004. Phone 1-800-SPRINGER, fax (201) 348-4505, e-mail orders-ny@springer-sbm.com, or visit www.springeronline.com. Apress Media, LLC is a Delaware LLC and the sole member (owner) is Springer Science + Business Media Finance Inc (SSBM Finance Inc). SSBM Finance Inc is a **Delaware** corporation.

For information on translations, please e-mail booktranslations@springernature.com; for reprint, paperback, or audio rights, please e-mail bookpermissions@springernature.com.

Apress titles may be purchased in bulk for academic, corporate, or promotional use. eBook versions and licenses are also available for most titles. For more information, reference our Print and eBook Bulk Sales web page at http://www.apress.com/bulk-sales.

Any source code or other supplementary material referenced by the author in this book is available to readers on GitHub. For more detailed information, please visit https://www.apress.com/gp/services/source-code.

To my wife, Lisa. Thank you for the room to work on my ideas and projects, and for always supporting me.

Table of Contents

About the Author

Simon Martinelli is a Java Champion, Vaadin Champion, and Oracle ACE Pro with over three decades of experience as a software architect, developer, consultant, and trainer. He is the creator of the AI Unified Process and a strong advocate of Spec-Driven Development.

As the owner of Martinelli LLC, he coaches teams to get up to speed with AI-driven development. He regularly shares his insights through international conferences, articles, and his blog Keep IT Simple, where he writes about AI, architecture, and modern Java development.

He is also a lecturer at two universities in Switzerland, where he teaches software architecture, persistence, DevOps, and cloud-native development.

About the Technical Reviewer

Neerja Bhatnagar is a software engineer with more than 19 years of experience building complex systems, including nine years building large-scale backend systems at a major tech company. She has an MS in Computer Science from California State University, Chico, and currently works at an early-stage startup focused on agent governance. Outside of work, Neerja enjoys pursuing her hobbies and spending time with friends and family.

Acknowledgments

Writing a book is never the work of one person alone. Many people helped me along the way, and I want to thank them here.

First, I want to thank the team at Apress who guided me through the whole process with patience and clear advice. I am grateful to my technical reviewer, who read the chapters with care and gave me honest and useful feedback. The book is stronger because of it.

I also want to thank the colleagues, clients, and friends in the community who tried the ideas in this book, asked hard questions, and shared their own experience. The AI Unified Process grew out of many real projects and many conversations. You know who you are.

And thank you to my wife Lisa for the patience and support.

Introduction

For more than thirty years I have built business software. I started with COBOL and moved to Java, and along the way, I learned one thing again and again: the hard part of software is rarely the code. The hard part is knowing what to build, writing it down clearly, and keeping that shared understanding alive as the system grows.

AI coding tools have changed how fast we can write code. They have not changed this hard part. In fact, they make it harder. When a tool can produce hundreds of lines in seconds, the risk is no longer slow typing. The risk is building the wrong thing quickly, with no clear record of what was intended or why.

This book is about a way to work that keeps the intent at the center. It is called the AI Unified Process. The idea is simple. We describe the behavior we want as clear specifications, we tie those specifications to tests, and we let AI do the heavy lifting of writing the code. The specification stays the source of truth. The code follows from it, and we can always check one against the other.

AI Unified Process builds on ideas that are not new. Use cases, introduced by Ivar Jacobson and refined by Alistair Cockburn, have helped teams capture behavior for a long time. What is new is how we connect these ideas to AI tools and to a working test suite, so the whole thing stays honest and stays in sync. The result is a process that works for new projects and for large existing systems, where most of us spend most of our time.

Who This Book Is For

This book is for developers, software architects, technical leads, but also requirements engineers and testers who want to use AI tools without losing control of their systems. You do not need to work with any single framework. The examples use the stack I know best, but the method does not depend on it. If you care about clear requirements, maintainable code, and software you can still understand a year from now, this book is for you.

How This Book Is Organized

The book follows the same path you would take on a real project, from the first question to a working system and then to a whole team.

Chapter 1 asks why we need spec-driven development at all, and what goes wrong without it. Chapter 2 gives you the AI Unified Process in a nutshell, so you have the full picture before we go into detail.

Chapters 3–6 are the core of the method. We move from requirements to specs (Chapter 3), learn to write specifications that can be executed (Chapter 4), turn those specs into tests (Chapter 5), and then let them drive the code (Chapter 6). This is the heart of the AI Unified Process: the specification stays the source of truth, and everything else follows from it.

Chapter 7 looks at the tools that support this way of working. Chapter 8 brings it all together in a case study, where we build a simple task manager step by step.

The last two chapters take you beyond a single project. Chapter 9 shows how to scale spec-driven development in teams. Chapter 10 collects the best practices and the common pitfalls, so you can learn from mistakes without making them yourself.

Each chapter builds on the one before it, but you can also jump to the topic you need.

A note on the approach

My guiding rule has always been to keep it simple. The AI Unified Process is not a heavy process with many roles and documents. It is a small set of practices that you can adopt one at a time. Start with one use case, write it down clearly, and let the rest grow from there.

Let us begin.

CHAPTER 1

Why Spec-Driven Development?

Code-first development often creates systems that are hard to understand, debug, maintain, and even harder to modernize. This chapter explains why this happens and how specifications as executable contracts restore clarity between business and IT.

From Balcony Architecture to Clarity

In many applications, code grows over years like a building with balconies added in different styles. Each "quick fix" or "urgent feature" adds another balcony. After a decade, the original structure is no longer visible. Developers must search through deeply nested conditions to understand what the system does. I call this "balcony architecture."

When modernizing such a system, the code is not the truth. It is only the result of many decisions over time. To rebuild or refactor safely, we must first understand the business rules and the real intent. Integration and unit tests might capture the correctness of behavior, but they do not also capture the decisions and the "why" of decisions. This knowledge should live in specifications, not in memories or comments.

S. Martinelli, *Spec-Driven Development*, Apress Pocket Guides,
https://doi.org/10.1007/979-8-8688-2851-5_1

My Aha Moment: Losing Track While Vibe-Coding

I experienced this problem myself when I built a volunteer management system. I used what is called vibe coding: asking AI tools for snippets and generating features quickly. It felt productive, but after some days, I had no overview anymore. The code existed, but the reasoning behind it did not. I could not answer simple questions about what was implemented and why.

This is where the AI Unified Process[1] was born. I threw away everything I had done so far and started from scratch, driven by specifications.

The AI Unified Process uses three lightweight artifacts:

- Requirements Catalog
- Entity Model
- System Use Cases

Requirements have three types:

- Functional requirements describe what the system should do and which capabilities it provides to users.
- Non-functional requirements define quality attributes such as performance, security, or availability.
- Constraints specify mandatory boundaries, for example, technology choices, architectural rules, or regulatory requirements.

The entity model not only defines the core domain concepts and their relationships but also serves as a glossary by establishing a shared, common, and consistent vocabulary for both business stakeholders and developers.

[1] `https://unifiedprocess.ai`

Finally, system use cases are the main executable contract between business intent and system behavior.

By keeping all artifacts under version control, I could trace my system again. I could check the specs to understand the current state, and I could validate AI-generated code against documented requirements. The project became manageable.

The AI Unified Process became my practical framework for spec-driven development: specifications as the single source of truth, with code and tests following them.

The Problem with Code-First

Most teams still start by opening the IDE and writing code. Documentation and tests are often added later, if at all. This approach may feel fast at the beginning, but it creates long-term problems. Documentation quickly becomes outdated because it is written separately from the code. Business rules are hidden inside implementations, spread across conditions, services, and database logic, and are hard to discover or explain.

Figure 1-1 illustrates a typical code-first workflow. Requirements are discussed informally, code is written immediately, and documentation and tests are added later, if at all. This ordering explains why intent is quickly lost once the system grows.

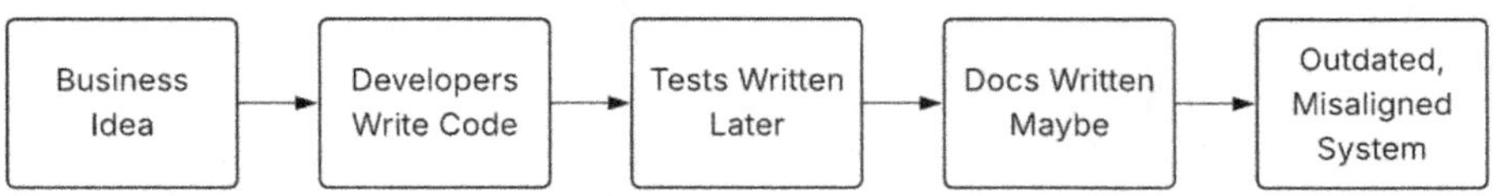

Figure 1-1. *The Code-First Workflow*

The diagram makes visible that code becomes the de facto source of truth, even though it was never designed to capture business intent

As the system grows, maintenance costs increase and debugging becomes more complex. Developers spend more time understanding existing behavior than adding new features. Misalignment between business and IT becomes common because the real rules live only in the code and in the heads of a few experienced team members. It also becomes harder to onboard a new developer to the system. New developers have to rely heavily on those few experienced team members to understand the system and implementation details. This creates more strain and work on the experienced team members, and also steepens the learning curve for the new members. Code can show how a system works from a technical perspective, but it rarely explains why the system behaves that way or which business decision led to a specific implementation.

What Spec-Driven Means

Spec-driven development turns this around. Instead of writing code first, teams start by writing specifications that describe the intended behavior of the system. These specifications define what the system should do before any implementation decisions are made. Code, tests, and documentation then follow the specification, not the other way around.

The core idea of spec-driven development is simple: the specification is the contract. Everything else flows from it. A specification describes behavior, domain concepts, and rules in a clear and structured way that both humans and tools can understand.

Figure 1-2 shows the inverted flow of spec-driven development. Specifications define behavior first, and code, tests, and documentation are derived from them.

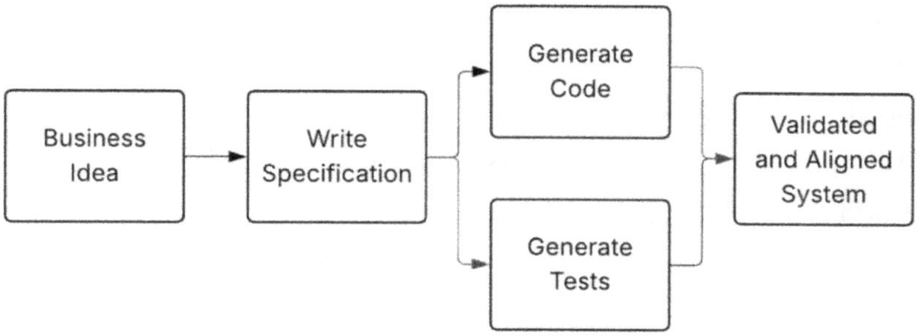

Figure 1-2. *The Spec-Driven Workflow*

This shift changes the role of code from "place where decisions are made" to "place where decisions are implemented."

Consider a simple example such as user login. A use case describes that a user logs in with valid credentials. The entity model defines what a user is, for example, a registered individual with an active account, identified by attributes such as ID, email, and role. Acceptance criteria specify important rules, such as denying access when credentials are invalid. Together, these elements define the contract of the feature.

From this contract, AI agents can scaffold the required code, generate tests for both success and failure scenarios, and keep documentation aligned with the actual behavior. The specification is no longer just a description written after implementation. It becomes the authoritative source that drives development and validation throughout the life cycle.

From Requirements to Use Cases

User stories are a good way to express business intent. They explain what a user wants and why. However, they intentionally avoid describing system behavior. Workflows, rules, edge cases, and error handling are often pushed into acceptance criteria or informal discussions.

System use cases build on top of this intent. They translate a requirement into observable system behavior. A use case makes explicit what the system does step by step when an actor interacts with it, including alternatives and failures. This turns vague intent into a precise and testable description of behavior.

This shift is important. Conversations move away from implementation details and focus on behavior. Teams discuss what must happen, under which conditions, and with which outcome. When business rules change, the use case is updated first. Code, tests, and documentation can then be adapted in a controlled and consistent way.

What Agile Left Behind

Agile methods successfully reduced heavy up-front documentation. This increased speed and flexibility. But it also removed durable, versioned descriptions of system behavior. In many teams, intent is scattered across user stories, tickets, comments, and wiki pages. Over time, these sources drift apart or become outdated.

User stories are great conversation starters, but they are not executable contracts. Acceptance criteria are often incomplete, inconsistent, or stored outside version control. As a result, there is no reliable place that describes what the system is supposed to do today.

The AI Unified Process closes this gap. Specifications are treated as first-class artifacts and stored in Git alongside the code. They evolve together with the implementation. This keeps agility, but restores clarity, traceability, and a stable source of truth that both humans and AI tools can rely on.

Why Now?

Specification-first development is not a new idea. Approaches such as model-driven development pursued similar goals in the past, but they largely failed in practice. The required notations were complicated and difficult to learn, the tools were complex, and teams often had to adopt the approach all at once. This created high entry barriers and made it hard to integrate these methods into everyday development work.

In practice, model-driven development often worked only up to a point. About 80% of the system could be generated from models, but the remaining 20% required manual work. This last part was usually the most complex and business-specific. As a result, teams had to mix generated code with hand-written extensions, which increased complexity, reduced maintainability, and broke the promise of full automation.

The AI Unified Process takes a much simpler and more pragmatic approach. Specifications are written as plain text in Markdown, using clear and structured language instead of formal modeling notations. There is no need for specialized modeling tools, and teams can adopt the approach incrementally, starting small and expanding over time.

What has changed is not the goal but the practicality of the approach and the urgency of getting it right. Generative AI has dramatically increased the speed at which code can be produced. Features that once took days can now be generated in minutes. But this increase in speed also increases risk. AI will confidently generate code even when requirements are ambiguous, incomplete, or wrong. Teams can now build the wrong solution faster than ever before.

This is especially visible in modernization projects. There, the main challenge is rarely writing new code. The harder part is understanding the business rules, constraints, and decisions that have accumulated over years. Without clear specifications, AI-generated code becomes just another layer added on top of already complex systems.

Modern AI systems can now understand structured natural language well enough to generate code, tests, and diagrams directly from specifications. This removes the need for complex modeling languages and makes specification-first development practical for real-world scenarios today. In the AI era, clear specifications are no longer just helpful documentation. They are the foundation that makes AI-assisted development safe, effective, and scalable.

Specifications As the Source of Truth

Figure 1-3 summarizes the central idea of spec-driven development: specifications sit at the center and drive all other artifacts.

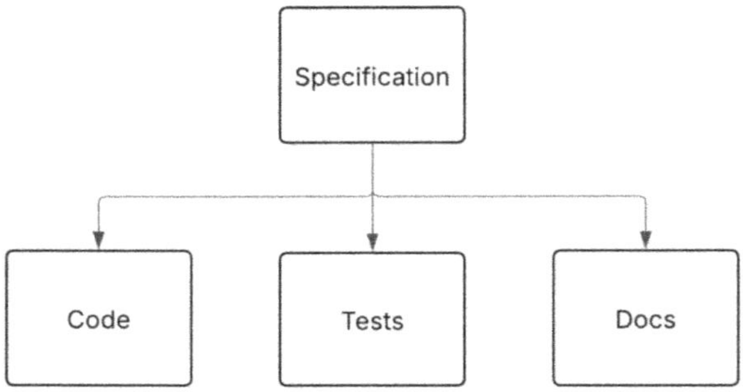

Figure 1-3. *Specifications as the Source of Truth*

Feedback flows back into the specification, but the specification always remains the authoritative reference.

Specifications sit at the center of the development process. They describe the intended system behavior, rules, and constraints in a precise and shared way. Code, tests, and documentation do not define the system independently. They are derived artifacts that are created from the same specifications and therefore stay consistent with each other.

The arrows in the diagram show this direction clearly: specifications drive implementation, validation, and documentation. Feedback from code or tests may lead to updates in the specifications, but the specification always remains the source of truth. This ensures that changes are intentional, traceable, and aligned with the original business intent.

Benefits of Spec-Driven Development

Alignment with Business

Spec-driven development improves alignment between business and IT because specifications are typically written in natural language (not programming language), which enables all stakeholders to read and understand and follow along. Requirements, use cases, and entity model describe what the system should do and why. Business stakeholders can review these specs early, confirm that they reflect their intent, and give feedback. This reduces misunderstandings and avoids situations where developers build the right solution for the wrong problem.

Reduced Rework

When specifications are written first, many errors are discovered before implementation begins. Ambiguous rules, missing cases, or incorrect assumptions become visible while writing use cases and acceptance criteria. Fixing a specification is much cheaper than fixing code, tests, and documentation later. Spec-driven development shifts problem detection to an earlier phase, which significantly reduces rework and late surprises.

Maintainability

Software systems change constantly. In a spec-driven approach, changes start in the specification, not in the code. When a requirement or business rule changes, the related specs are updated first. From there, code, tests, and documentation can be regenerated or adapted consistently. This makes change predictable and controlled. Instead of digging through code to understand the impact, teams can rely on up-to-date specifications as the starting point.

Living Documentation

In many projects, documentation becomes outdated because it is written manually and maintained separately from the code. With spec-driven development, specifications are part of the development workflow and stored in version control. They are updated whenever behavior changes. Because code and tests are derived from specs, the documentation stays current by design. This creates true living documentation that reflects the real state of the system at any time.

Efficiency

Spec-driven development improves developer efficiency by reducing repetitive and low-value work. Clear specifications allow tools and AI agents to generate scaffolding, boilerplate code, and test stubs automatically. Developers can focus on architecture, business logic, edge cases, and quality instead of translating vague requirements into structure. The result is faster development with better consistency and fewer errors, especially in complex or long-running projects. Efficiency is also achieved because clear specifications provide means for better communication with less confusion and because they are an unambiguous source of truth.

Modernization Ready

Spec-driven development makes systems future-proof and easier to modernize. Because behavior, rules, and domain concepts are captured in technology-independent specifications, the system is not tightly coupled to a specific framework, language, or platform. When a new technology stack is needed, for example, moving from a legacy system to a modern architecture, the existing specifications can be reused as the foundation.

Instead of reverse-engineering business logic from old code, teams can regenerate the system from the specs using new tools, frameworks, or AI agents. This reduces risk and effort in modernization projects. The specification remains stable while implementations can change. Spec-driven development therefore protects business knowledge from technical churn and makes long-term evolution possible without starting from scratch.

Misconceptions

Specs Slow Us Down

A common belief is that writing specifications first adds overhead and delays development. In practice, the opposite is true. Teams always spend time clarifying requirements, fixing misunderstandings, and correcting wrong implementations. Spec-driven development simply moves this effort to an earlier point, where it is much cheaper. By resolving open questions before coding starts, teams avoid rework, reduce interruptions, and make development flow more smoothly.

Specs Are Just Documents

Another misconception is that specifications are only documentation. In spec-driven development, specs are executable artifacts. They drive code generation, test creation, and validation. Use cases, requirements, and acceptance criteria act as contracts that tools and AI agents can interpret. This makes specifications an active part of the system, not static text that quickly becomes outdated.

We Have No Time

Teams often say they do not have time to write specifications. In reality, the time is already being spent, though in less visible ways. It appears as meetings to clarify behavior, debugging sessions to understand hidden rules, and repeated explanations to new team members. Spec-driven development does not add extra work. It shifts the work to the beginning, where it reduces overall effort and creates long-term savings.

Why This Matters Now

Generative AI has dramatically increased the speed at which code can be produced. Features that once took days can now be generated in minutes. However, faster coding also increases risk when the underlying intent is unclear. AI will confidently generate code even when requirements are ambiguous or wrong. This means teams can now build the wrong solution faster than ever before.

Modernization projects clearly show that speed alone is not the main problem. The real challenge is understanding existing business rules, constraints, and decisions that have accumulated over time. Without clear specifications, AI-generated code becomes just another layer added on top of already complex systems. Spec-driven development provides the necessary structure by making intent explicit before automation begins. In the AI era, clear specifications are not optional. They are the foundation that allows AI to be used safely, effectively, and at scale.

Key Takeaways

Code-first development often leads to fragile systems that are difficult to understand, change, and modernize over time. Spec-driven development addresses this problem by placing specifications at the center of the development process and treating them as the primary source of truth. Advances in AI make executable specifications practical, allowing code, tests, and documentation to be derived directly from clearly written intent. As a result, teams benefit from better alignment with the business, improved maintainability, and higher overall efficiency.

The next chapters show how to apply these ideas in practice using the AI Unified Process.

CHAPTER 2

The AI Unified Process in a Nutshell

Chapter 1 explained why spec-driven development matters. This chapter introduces the AI Unified Process.[1] The AI Unified Process is a lightweight method that uses simple artifacts and AI assistance to make specifications the foundation of development.

Why a Process at All?

Modern development still suffers from unclear requirements and missing specifications. Agile improved speed, but it did not solve the problem of fragmented and outdated intent.

AI can generate code fast, but without precise specifications it generates the wrong thing faster.

The AI Unified Process brings structure by making specifications the single source of truth. The AI Unified Process is inspired by Rational Unified Process (RUP) but redesigned for modern workflows, without heavy modeling but with simple artifacts, continuous iteration, and AI-assisted refinement.

---

[1] `https://unifiedprocess.ai`

S. Martinelli, *Spec-Driven Development*, Apress Pocket Guides,
https://doi.org/10.1007/979-8-8688-2851-5_2

Core Principles of the AI Unified Process

The AI Unified Process follows a small set of principles that guide how specifications are written, structured, and used in daily work. These principles ensure that specifications stay clear, lightweight, and usable by both humans and AI tools.

Executable Specifications

Specifications in the AI Unified Process are written so they can be used directly for automation. A specification is not finished when it is only readable but when it is precise enough to drive code generation, test scaffolding, or validation. System use cases describe observable system behavior with clear steps and outcomes. This makes them suitable as executable contracts. Executability does not require formal languages. It requires structured text, clear intent, and unambiguous behavior.

Minimalism

The AI Unified Process creates only the artifacts that are truly needed. Each artifact must add clarity or enable automation. If it does not, it should not exist. AI Unified Process focuses on three core artifacts in a fixed order: requirements, entity model, and system use cases. This avoids documentation overload and keeps maintenance effort low. Minimalism makes the AI Unified Process easy to adopt and sustainable over time.

Traceability by Design

Traceability is built into the AI Unified Process from the beginning. Requirements and system use cases use stable and unique identifiers. These identifiers are referenced across artifacts, code, tests, and commits. This creates a clear path from business intent to implementation and back. Traceability is not added later by tools. It emerges naturally from how specifications are written and linked.

AI Collaboration

AI supports the work, but humans stay in control. AI can help summarize workshop results, draft requirements, expand them into use cases, and check consistency. Clear specifications reduce ambiguity and guide AI tools effectively. Instead of guessing, AI works within explicit boundaries defined by the specs. Humans always review and decide.

Version-Controlled Everything

All AI Unified Process artifacts live in Git, just like source code. Requirements, entity models, and use cases evolve together with the implementation. Every change is visible, reviewable, and reversible. This prevents outdated documentation and enables automation, collaboration, and long-term maintainability.

Together, these principles make the AI Unified Process practical and lightweight. Specifications become living, executable contracts that guide development without introducing heavy processes or complex tooling.

The AI Unified Process Diagram

The AI Unified Process is a continuous process. Work does not move from one stage to the next in a linear way. Instead, teams iterate in short cycles. They specify requirements, entity models, and use cases, generate code or tests with AI support, validate the results against the specs, review them as a team, and then refine both specs and implementation together.

Figure 2-1 shows the AI Unified Process as a continuous loop rather than a linear sequence.

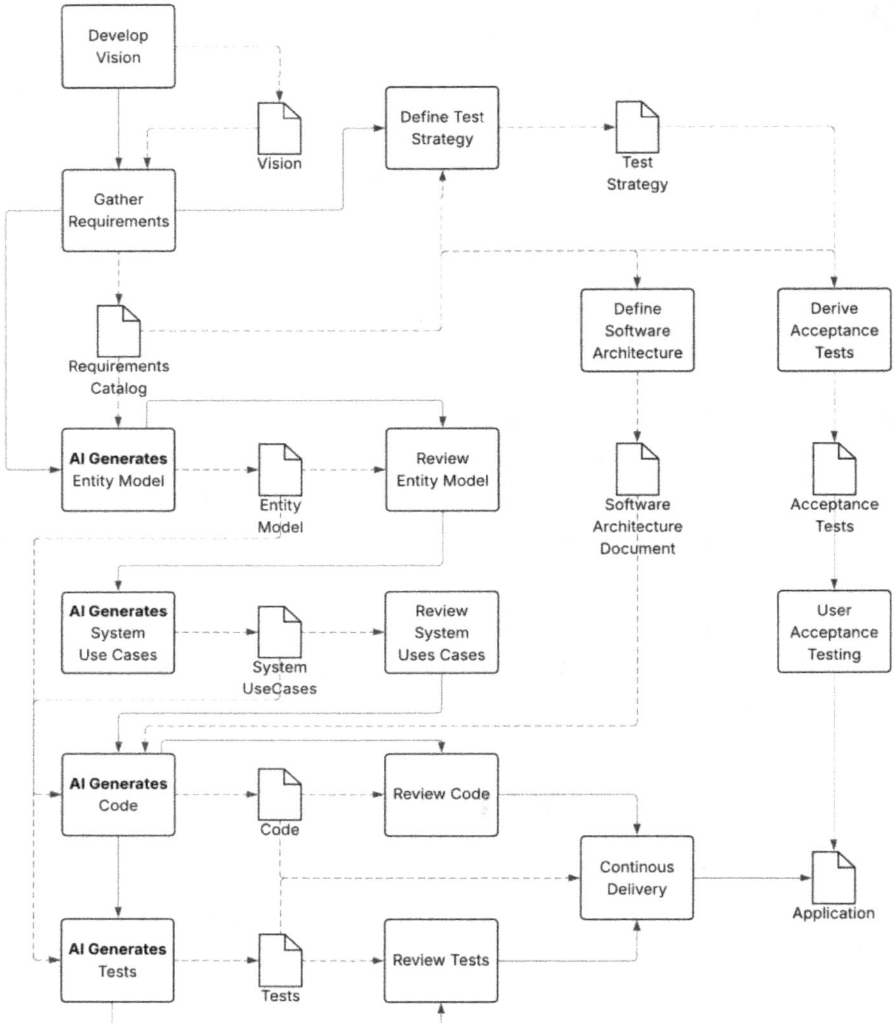

***Figure 2-1.** The AI Unified Process*

The AI Unified Process Artifacts

The AI Unified Process defines three core artifacts, known as the Specification Core:

- Requirements Catalog
- Entity Model
- System Use Cases

Requirements Catalog

Requirements are stored in a lightweight table format and have stable identifiers. There are three different types:

- **Functional Requirements (FR-###)**: Describe system capabilities and user-facing behavior
- **Non-Functional Requirements (NFR-###)**: Define quality attributes such as performance, availability, and security
- **Constraints (C-###)**: Define mandatory boundaries such as technology choices, architecture rules, or regulation

Every requirement receives a stable ID. These IDs create the traceability chain between intent, specs, code, and tests.

Functional Requirements are typically expressed as User Stories, which captures business intent. System use cases then expand these requirements into executable specifications.

Entity Model

The entity model defines the core domain concepts and their relationships. It captures the nouns of the system and provides a shared structure for requirements and system use cases. In the AI Unified Process, entity models are intentionally simple and focus on what matters, not on technical details. It also serves as a glossary.

Diagrams-as-code (e.g., Mermaid or PlantUML) are used to visualize entities and their relationships in a lightweight and readable way. This makes the model easy to understand and easy to maintain. Entity names are used consistently in requirements and use cases, which creates implicit traceability without introducing additional identifiers. This helps both humans and AI tools understand how behavior relates to domain data.

System Use Cases

System use cases describe system behavior in a structured and observable way. They explain what the system does when an actor interacts with it, including normal flows, alternatives, and error situations. This makes behavior explicit instead of hiding it in code or informal notes.

Each system use case links back to one or more requirements and references the relevant entities by name. This creates a clear connection between business intent, domain concepts, and system behavior. System use cases are the main executable specification in the AI Unified Process. They provide the precision needed for AI tools and developers to generate code, tests, and validations.

Every use case has a stable UC-xxx identifier and is stored as its own Markdown file. This keeps use cases small, focused, version-controlled, and easy to review and evolve over time.

User Stories vs. System Use Cases

The AI Unified Process uses both User Stories and System use cases, but they serve different purposes.

User Stories capture business intent. They describe *why* a user wants something, not *how the system behaves.* They are short, easy to read, and ideal for early discussions.

Example structure:

As a … I want … so that …

This format helps stakeholders' express goals without thinking about system behavior.

System use cases expand this intent into an executable specification.

They describe *what the system does* when the actor performs an action, including flows, conditions, and results.

Use Cases bring clarity that AI tools and developers need to generate and validate code.

In the AI Unified Process:

- User Stories → express *intent*
- System Use Cases → define *behavior*

User Stories start the conversation. Use Cases formalize it into an executable contract.

Version Control and Traceability

All AI Unified Process artifacts are Markdown files stored in Git. IDs remain stable and create a traceability chain.

ID Formats

- FR-### for Functional Requirements
- NFR-### for Non-Functional Requirements
- C-### for Constraints
- UC-### for System Use Cases

This creates durable links across specifications, code, and tests.

Version Control Practices

All AI Unified Process artifacts are stored as plain Markdown files in a Git repository. This makes specifications part of the normal development workflow and treats them with the same discipline as source code. Markdown is readable for humans, easy to diff, and well supported by tools and AI systems.

Each artifact type can have its own clear folder structure. A typical setup looks like this:

```
/specs
  entity_model.md
  requirements_catalog.md
  use_cases.puml
  /usecases
    UC-001_assign_task.md
    UC-002_complete_task.md
```

This structure keeps artifacts easy to find and supports a clear flow from requirements to entity model to system use cases.

Benefits of versioning specs in Git:

- Complete history of every change, including who changed what, when, and why.

- Easy branching and merging, so teams can evolve specs collaboratively.
- Direct links between commits, pull requests, and specification updates.
- AI tools can analyze diffs to detect inconsistencies, outdated behavior, or missing updates.

By keeping specifications in Git, they stay current, reviewable, and tightly connected to the code they drive.

Traceability

Traceability ensures that every behavior can be linked back to intent. It connects what stakeholders want with what the system actually does. In the AI Unified Process, traceability is not an afterthought or a manual activity. It is built into the structure of the specifications from the beginning.

Figure 2-2 illustrates how all artifacts relate to each other. Functional Requirements, Non-Functional Requirements, and Constraints express intent and boundaries. These requirements inspire system use cases, which describe concrete system behavior. Use Cases reference domain entities and serve as the bridge between intent and implementation. From there, code and tests are created, always pointing back to the originating Use Case.

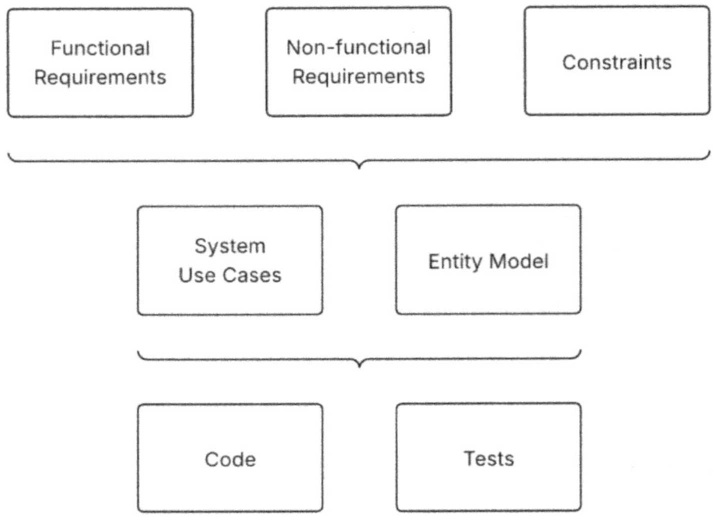

Figure 2-2. *Traceability Map*

Figure 2-2 visualizes how the AI Unified Process establishes traceability across requirements, use cases, code, and tests.

AI Unified Process traceability makes navigation easy. A team member can start with a user goal, follow the linked Use Case, and quickly find the relevant code and tests. The same path works in reverse. When code changes, it is immediately clear which behavior and which business intent might be affected.

Traceability is achieved through stable references across artifacts:

- Each system use case lists the related requirement IDs.
- Entities are referenced by name inside use cases.
- Tests and code comments link back to use case IDs.

Because these links are explicit and machine-readable, AI agents can automatically work with them. They can

- Verify coverage and detect missing implementations
- Identify outdated specifications when code evolves
- Generate traceability matrices or compliance reports

With the AI Unified Process, traceability is lightweight but powerful. It ensures that code can be traced back to its original intent, keeping specifications, implementation, and business goals continuously aligned.

The AI Unified Process Life Cycle

The AI Unified Process defines a simple, repeating life cycle that keeps specifications and implementation in sync. The life cycle is intentionally short and continuous. There are no fixed phases or handovers. Teams move through these steps as often as needed, sometimes several times per day. Figure 2-3 breaks the AI Unified Process loop into five recurring activities: specify, generate, validate, review, and refine.

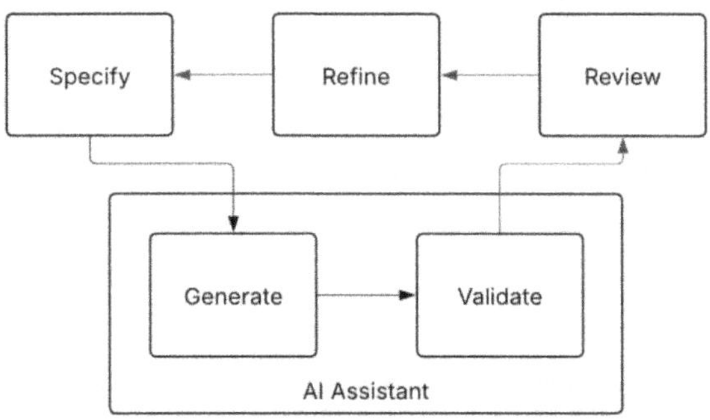

Figure 2-3. *AI Unified Process Life cycle*

Specify

The team captures intent and structure. This includes updating the requirements catalog, refining system use cases, and adjusting the entity model. The goal is not completeness but enough clarity to describe what the system should do next. Specifications are written in simple, structured language so they can be understood by both humans and AI tools.

Generate

AI tools use the specifications as input to generate code scaffolds, test stubs, and diagrams. This step focuses on speed and consistency. Generated artifacts provide a starting point, not a final solution, and always reflect the current state of the specifications.

Validate

Generated and existing code is checked against the specifications. Tests verify that use case flows and business rules are implemented correctly. Validation can be automated in CI pipelines, ensuring that changes in code or specs do not break the agreed behavior.

Review

Humans review both specifications and generated artifacts. This step ensures correctness, readability, and architectural quality. AI assists, but humans remain responsible for decisions, trade-offs, and final approval.

Refine

Based on feedback from validation and review, the team updates specifications and code together. Ambiguities are removed, rules are clarified, and edge cases are added. Nothing is changed in isolation.

The life cycle then repeats. With each iteration, specifications become more precise, implementation becomes more stable, and the risk of misunderstandings and rework is reduced.

How the AI Unified Process Compares to Rational Unified Process

The AI Unified Process is inspired by the Rational Unified Process (RUP) but redesigned for modern workflows, lightweight specs, and AI collaboration. The table below highlights the conceptual differences.

The AI Unified Process is the lightweight, modern version of what RUP tried to achieve. Table 2-1 compares the processes.

Table 2-1. *RUP vs. AI Unified Process*

Aspect	Rational Unified Process	AI Unified Process
Specification style	UML models and structured documents	Structured Markdown specs
Tools	Heavy modeling tools	Git, docs-as-code, diagram-as-code, AI agents
Process structure	Four phases (Inception, Elaboration, Construction, Transition)	Continuous iteration
Artifact weight	Many artifacts and roles	Minimal, interconnected artifacts
Automation	Limited, mostly manual	AI-assisted generation and consistency checking
Traceability	Requires discipline and tooling	Built-in through IDs and AI assistance
Adoption	Steep learning curve	Incremental, low barrier to entry

Why the AI Unified Process Works Now

The AI Unified Process would not have worked 20 years ago. The ideas behind specification-first development already existed, but the environment was not ready. Today, three fundamental changes make the AI Unified Process practical and effective.

AI Can Interpret Structured Natural Language

Modern AI systems can understand structured natural language with a high level of accuracy. Requirements and system use cases written in simple, precise prose are no longer just for humans. AI agents can read them, reason about them, and use them as input for generation and validation. This removes the need for heavy formal modeling languages such as UML, which were difficult to write, hard to maintain, and often disconnected from real development work.

Automation Is Ubiquitous

Automation is now a standard part of software development. CI pipelines, automated tests, and quality checks are available in almost every project. The AI Unified Process integrates specifications directly into these workflows. Specs can be validated automatically, checked for consistency, and compared against code on every change. This makes specifications living artifacts instead of static documents.

Lightweight Tools Replace Heavy Modeling

Instead of specialized modeling tools, the AI Unified Process relies on tools developers already use every day:

- Doc-as-Code using Markdown or AsciiDoc
- Diagram-as-Code using PlantUML and Mermaid.js
- Version control for tracking and collaboration
- AI assistants for generation, validation, and refactoring

These tools are simple, text-based, and easy to integrate. They lower the entry barrier and allow teams to adopt the AI Unified Process incrementally.

Together, these three factors change the economics of specifications. Executable specifications are no longer expensive to create or maintain. They become practical, accessible, and sustainable, even for small teams and fast-moving projects.

Summary

The AI Unified Process provides a simple but powerful structure for spec-driven development. It focuses on clarity and discipline without introducing unnecessary complexity.

It is built on clear principles that define how specifications are written, versioned, and used as executable contracts. These principles ensure that intent is captured before implementation and stays visible over time.

The AI Unified Process relies on three core artifacts. Requirements capture intent, the Entity Model describes the domain and ensures a shared language, and system use cases define behavior. Together, they form a complete and lightweight specification set.

An iterative life cycle keeps specifications and implementation aligned. Teams specify, generate, validate, review, and refine in short cycles. There are no phases or handovers, only continuous learning and improvement.

Built-in traceability connects every artifact. Stable identifiers link requirements, use cases, code, and tests. This makes it easy to understand why something exists, what it affects, and what must change when requirements evolve.

Finally, the AI Unified Process is a practical, AI-ready process. Specifications are written in structured natural language that AI tools can read and use. AI assists with generation and validation, while humans stay in control of decisions and quality.

The next chapter shows how to turn these concepts into real specifications, with concrete examples, templates, and diagrams that you can apply directly in your own projects.

CHAPTER 3

From Requirements to Specs

This chapter explains how to move from raw ideas to structured specifications. It shows how to create the three AI Unified Process[1] artifacts and how AI tools help summarize, extract, classify, and validate requirements.

From Ideas to Specifications

Every project begins with conversations. Stakeholders share goals, ideas, concerns, and sometimes contradictory expectations. On their own, these inputs are informal and unstable and change often. The first task in spec-driven development is to turn this raw input into clear specifications that can be reviewed, versioned, and evolved over time. This shift from discussion to written specs creates a shared understanding and removes ambiguity early, before code is written.

The AI Unified Process uses three core specification artifacts for this purpose. Requirements describe what the system must achieve and which constraints apply. The Entity Model defines the domain concepts and establishes a shared language. System use cases describe how the

[1] 1 https://unifiedprocess.ai

S. Martinelli, *Spec-Driven Development*, Apress Pocket Guides,
https://doi.org/10.1007/979-8-8688-2851-5_3

system behaves in concrete, observable steps. Together, these artifacts form an executable specification suite. They are precise enough to guide developers and AI tools, yet simple enough to stay readable and maintainable. From this foundation, code, tests, and documentation can be generated and validated in a consistent way.

Gathering Requirements with the Help of AI

Workshops and collaborative requirement-gathering sessions remain a central part of the process. Methods such as domain storytelling and event storming help teams understand how the business really works. They make workflows visible, uncover business rules, highlight exceptions, and surface the terms that stakeholders actually use. These sessions create a shared mental model that cannot be produced by tools alone. The direct interaction between business experts and the software development team is where most insights are created.

AI does not replace this human collaboration. Its role starts after the workshop. Transcripts, notes, photos of boards, and documented stories can be used as input for AI tools. AI can summarize discussions, extract candidate requirements, identify rules and constraints, and help structure the results into a first version of the requirements catalog, entity model, and use cases. This reduces manual effort and speeds up consolidation, while the team remains responsible for reviewing, correcting, and approving the final specifications.

AI-Assisted Requirement Capturing

The requirements capturing process starts with the workshop output. These workshops are typically collaborative discovery sessions, often inspired by Domain-Driven Design (DDD). Common formats include Domain Storytelling, where stakeholders describe their daily work as sequences of actions, and Event Storming, where domain events, commands, and policies are explored on a timeline.

The output of these workshops includes domain stories, event storming boards, flip charts, digital whiteboards, transcripts, and personal notes. At this stage, the information is intentionally raw and unstructured. It reflects how stakeholders talk about their work, which is valuable, but it is not yet suitable as a specification. Figure 3-1 outlines the transition from raw workshop output to a structured requirements catalog.

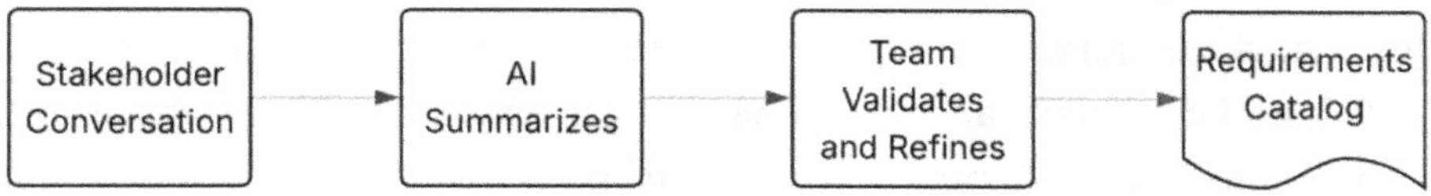

Figure 3-1. *Requirements Capturing*

In the summarization step, AI tools are used to condense this raw material into a clear and readable list of statements. Redundant explanations are removed, long discussions are shortened, and the core messages are preserved. The result is a set of candidate requirements and observations that represent the workshop outcomes without losing important context.

Next comes extraction. Here, AI analyzes the summarized text and identifies different kinds of information. It separates goals from concrete rules, detects quality expectations such as performance or security, and highlights explicit or implicit constraints. This step helps ensure that important non-functional aspects and boundaries are not overlooked.

During classification, the extracted items are grouped into Functional Requirements, Non-Functional Requirements, and Constraints. Each item can then receive a stable identifier and be placed in the requirements catalog. This creates structure and makes the results traceable and usable for later steps such as writing use cases and tests.

Human Review As the Critical Quality Gate

Finally, human review is not optional. It is the most critical step in the entire AI-assisted requirements process. AI can summarize, extract, and structure information efficiently, but it cannot take responsibility for correctness, intent, or shared understanding. Only the team can do that. During review, the team actively validates the AI-generated results: duplicates are merged, contradictions are resolved, missing rules are added, and unclear or ambiguous wording is rewritten. This is where assumptions are challenged and intent is made explicit.

In practice, this step is often skipped or rushed. Teams trust the structured output because it "looks complete." This is a dangerous illusion. When proper human review is missing, several problems typically appear later in the project:

- False confidence

  The specification appears structured and professional, but it contains subtle misunderstandings. These errors are harder to detect later because they are now documented and implicitly trusted.

- Hidden contradictions

  AI often preserves conflicting statements from different workshop inputs. Without review, these conflicts move downstream into use cases, tests, and code, where they cause inconsistent behavior.

- Ambiguous behavior

  Vague wording that humans would normally clarify in conversation remains in the spec. AI will still generate code from it, but each generation may interpret the ambiguity differently.

- Misaligned automation

  AI agents follow the written specification exactly. If the spec is wrong, incomplete, or unclear, the automation will reliably produce the wrong result, faster and at larger scale.

- Loss of shared understanding

  The real value of requirements workshops is not the raw output but the shared mental model created during discussion. Without review, this shared understanding never makes it into the written artifacts, and knowledge remains implicit and fragile.

A good review is therefore not a proofreading exercise. It is a deliberate alignment step. The team confirms that the written requirements truly reflect what was discussed, agreed upon, and intended. Disagreements are resolved now, while they are still cheap to fix.

The workshop remains the primary source of domain knowledge. AI reduces manual effort and accelerates structuring, but human review turns structured text into a reliable specification.

The outcome of this step is a requirements set that is

- Correct and unambiguous
- Shared and agreed upon
- Internally consistent
- Reviewable and version-controlled
- Safe to use as input for use cases, tests, and AI-driven code generation

Without this step, spec-driven development degrades into automated guesswork. With it, specifications become a stable foundation that the rest of the AI Unified Process can safely build on.

Example Requirements Catalog

Each requirement receives a unique and immutable ID, following the conventions described in Chapter 2. These IDs enable traceability across use cases, code, and tests.

Table 3-1 shows an example of a requirements catalog.

Table 3-1. *Example Requierments Catalog*

ID	Title	Description
FR-001	Assign Task	As a user, I want to assign a task to another user so that work can be distributed.
NFR-001	Task Response Time	Task operations must complete in under one second.
C-001	Platform Constraint	Backend must run on Java 21 and PostgreSQL 16.

Entity Models As Foundations

Entity Models define the nouns of the system. They provide the shared language for requirements and system use cases. In the AI Unified Process, the entity model also replaces a traditional glossary. Each entity name represents a domain term. Optional short descriptions clarify meaning and avoid misunderstandings.

System use cases and requirements reference entities by name; that way, terminology stays consistent automatically. There is no separate glossary to maintain.

This keeps the specification minimal while still providing a clear vocabulary for humans and AI tools.

Figure 3-2 shows the entity model for the task manager example, and Tables 3-2 and 3-3 define the details of each entity in the diagram.

Figure 3-2. *Entity Model*

Table 3-2. *User Entity Attributes*

Attribute	Data type	Length	Validation rules
ID	UUID	36	Required, unique, immutable
name	String	100	Required, not empty
email	String	255	Required, unique, valid email format
active	Boolean	–	Required, default true

Table 3-3. *Task Entity Attributes*

Attribute	Data type	Length	Validation rules
ID	UUID	36	Required, unique, immutable
description	String	500	Required, not empty
dueDate	Date	–	Optional, must be today or in the future
Status	Enum	–	Required, allowed values: OPEN, ASSIGNED, DONE

User
A registered person who can create and be assigned tasks.

Task
A unit of work with a description, due date, and status.

This level of detail keeps the entity model simple but precise enough for validation, database design, and AI-assisted generation.

From Requirements to System Use Cases

Functional Requirements express user intent at a high level. They describe what a user wants to achieve, without defining detailed behavior.

System use cases expand this intent into structured, testable behavior.

Example:

- Requirement FR-001: User can assign a task.
- Use Case UC-001: Assign Task

Use Cases describe the concrete interaction steps, alternatives, and error cases. They act as the main executable specification that drives code, tests, and validation.

Writing Clear Use Cases

A System Use Case describes one interaction between an external actor and the system that leads to a meaningful result.

Use Case Diagram

The AI Unified Process uses UML Use Case diagrams to show the system scope from a user perspective. The diagram is written in PlantUML because Mermaid doesn't have a use case diagram type. That way it can be stored in Git, reviewed in pull requests, and regenerated consistently. It gives a quick overview of which actors interact with the system and which system capabilities exist, without going into workflow details.

The Use Case Diagram complements the system use cases. The diagram answers "what does the system offer" at a glance, while each system use case (UC-###) describes the detailed, testable behavior with main flow, alternate flows, and exceptions. In practice, the diagram is often generated or updated from the list of use cases, so it stays aligned with the specification files.

Figure 3-3 provides a high-level overview of system capabilities from a user perspective. The diagram complements, but does not replace, the detailed system use cases.

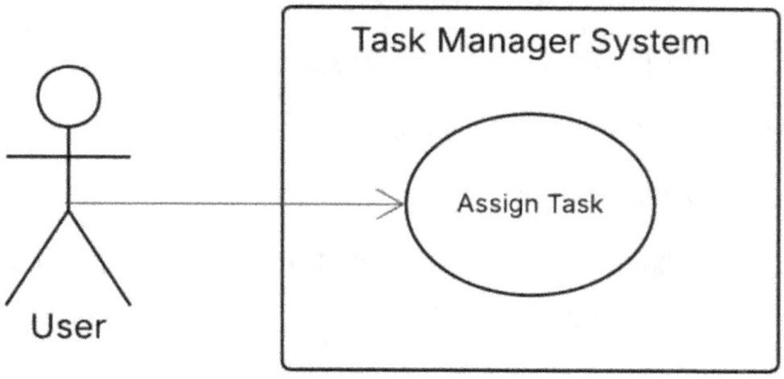

Figure 3-3. *Use Case Assign Task*

Structure of a System Use Case

A typical AI Unified Process use case contains the elements presented in Table 3-4.

Table 3-4. *Use Case Structure*

Field	Purpose
ID	Unique identifier (e.g., UC-001)
Title	Short description of the goal
Actor(s)	External roles interacting with the system
Goal	Expected outcome
Status	Draft, Reviewed, Approved
Preconditions	Conditions and/or state that must be true before the interaction starts

(*continued*)

Table 3-4. *(continued)*

Field	Purpose
Trigger	Event that starts the use case
Main flow	Ordered steps of the successful path
Alternate flows	Variations that still end in success
Exception flows	Failures or error paths
Postconditions	Conditions and/or state that must be true after the interaction completes successfully
Business rules	Rules applied during execution
Linked requirements	IDs such as FR-001, NFR-001, C-001

Example Use Case

```
**Use Case:** UC-001 Assign Task
**Actor:** User
**Goal:** Assign a task to another active user
**Status:** Documented
**Preconditions:**
- User is authenticated
- Task exists and is unassigned
**Trigger:**
- User selects "Assign Task"
**Main Flow:**
System displays the task details and list of active users.
User selects a target user.
System validates the target user is active.
System assigns the task.
```

```
System notifies the target user and confirms success.
Alternate Flow:
3a. Target user is inactive
    System shows error and returns to step 2.
Exception Flow:
4a. Database unavailable
    System logs the error and informs the user.
Postconditions:
- Task is assigned to the selected active user.
- Target user is notified.
Linked Requirements: FR-001, NFR-001, C-001
```

Activity Diagram of the Main Flow

Figure 3-4 illustrates the main success flow of the "Assign Task" use case as an activity diagram. It makes decision points and flow alternatives visible at a glance.

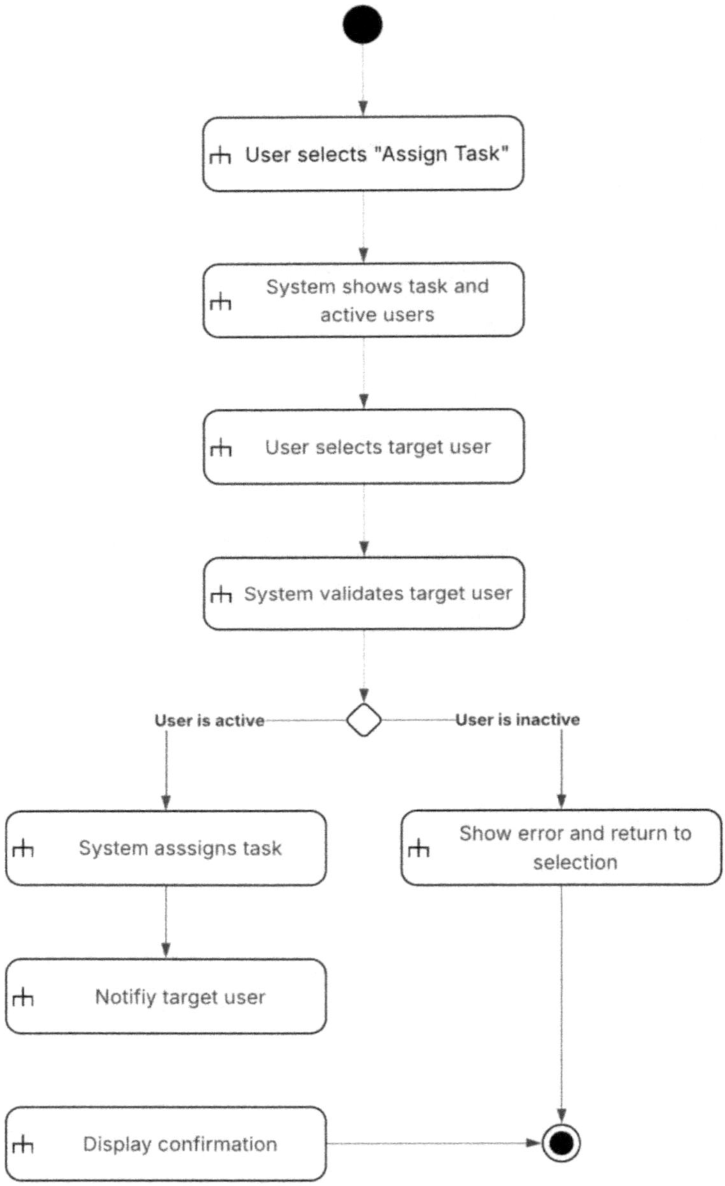

Figure 3-4. *Activity Diagram of Main Flow*

Writing Good Flows

There are a few important recommendations to write good flows:

Keep steps observable.

Each step should describe something that can be seen or verified from outside the system. Avoid internal implementation details. Write what the system does or shows, not how it is implemented.

Use active voice.

Clearly state who performs the action. Use "System displays ..." or "User selects ..." instead of vague phrasing. This improves readability and avoids ambiguity for both humans and AI tools.

Reference the step number in alternate and exception flows.

Alternate and exception flows must point back to the exact step where they diverge. This keeps the flow easy to follow and makes it clear which condition changes the normal behavior.

One goal per use case.

A system use case should focus on a single, meaningful outcome. If multiple goals appear, split them into separate use cases. This keeps use cases small, focused, and easier to test and maintain.

Relationships Between Use Cases

UML Use Case Diagrams support relationships. Table 3-5 shows the different types of relationships.

Table 3-5. *Use Case Relationships*

Relationship	Meaning	Example
Include	Reusable sub-flow used by multiple use cases	Authenticate User included in many flows
Extend	Optional behavior that adds steps	Add 2FA extends Login
Generalization	Specialized version of a parent use case	Submit Order → Submit Bulk Order

> **Important** Relationships in use case diagrams are sometimes hard to understand. Only use relationships when they add clarity.

Metadata and Traceability

Use Case metadata enables AI-assisted checks. This allows for the traceability from the requirements to the code and tests as shown in Figure 3-5.

Example:

```
id: UC-001
name: Assign Task
actors:
  - User
linkedRequirements:
  - FR-001
  - NFR-001
  - C-001
entities:
  - User
  - Task
```

```
postconditions:
  - Task assigned to target user
  - Target user notified
```

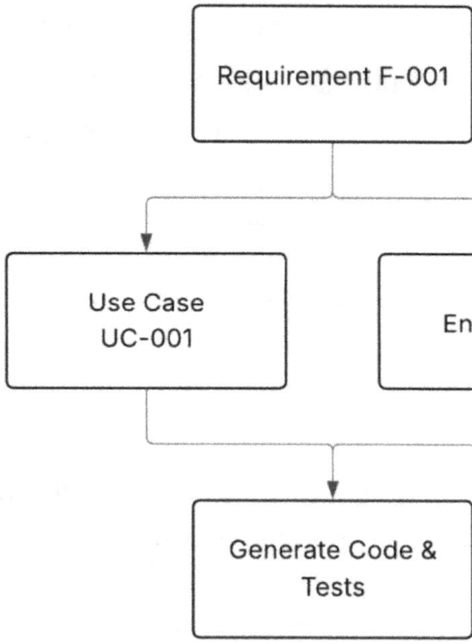

Figure 3-5. *Traceability Chain*

AI Assistance in Writing and Validating Use Cases

AI tools support the entire Use Case life cycle. Table 3-6 describes the AI assistance activities.

Table 3-6. *AI Assitance Activities*

Activity	AI support
Drafting	Expands user stories into structured use cases
Validation	Checks coverage of linked requirements
Consistency	Aligns terminology with entity model definitions
Diagramming	Generates PlantUML and Mermaid diagrams
Refactoring	Detects duplicates or overlaps

Humans remain in control and verify intent and correctness.

Summary

In this chapter, we have seen how the core artifacts of the AI Unified Process work together to form a coherent specification set. Requirements describe intent by capturing what the system must achieve and which constraints apply, without going into detailed behavior. They provide the business goals and boundaries that guide all further work.

System use cases build on this intent and describe behavior. They turn abstract goals into concrete, observable, and testable workflows that explain how the system reacts to user actions, including alternatives and error situations.

What makes a system use case testable is its structure. Preconditions define the required setup. The main flow describes the expected success path step by step. Alternate and exception flows describe valid variations and failures. Postconditions define the observable outcome that must be true after execution. Together, these elements define clear acceptance criteria that can be verified manually or automated as tests.

Entity models complement this by creating shared structure. They define the domain concepts and vocabulary that are used consistently across requirements and use cases. Because use cases reference entities by name, tests and implementations use the same terms and concepts, ensuring that everyone talks about the same things in the same way and verifies the same behavior.

Together, these artifacts form the executable specification suite of the AI Unified Process. They are precise enough to guide developers and AI tools, while remaining lightweight and readable for humans. AI tools support this work by helping to capture, refine, and validate specifications through summarization, extraction, consistency checks, and generation, while humans stay in control of intent and decisions. Built-in traceability links everything back to business purpose through stable identifiers and explicit references, ensuring that behavior, code, and tests can always be traced to the original intent.

The next chapter explains how to turn these specifications into executable contracts.

CHAPTER 4

Writing Executable Specifications

In the previous chapters, we introduced the core artifacts of the AI Unified Process:[1] requirements, the entity model, and system use cases. We saw what each artifact is for and how they work together to turn business intent into structured specifications. This chapter moves from structure to craft. The question is no longer what a system use case is but how to write one well.

A use case only becomes useful when it is precise enough that different people read it and reach the same understanding. Developers should understand what to implement. Testers should understand what to verify. Business stakeholders should recognize the intended behavior. AI tools should be able to derive code and tests from it without filling in missing meanings on their own.

Executable specifications are contracts, not code. They describe observable system behavior with enough precision that implementation and verification can follow without guesswork. This clarity must exist before coding starts, because ambiguity does not disappear, it moves downstream into code reviews, failed tests, production defects, and long clarification meetings. Many teams already write documentation that is readable, but readable is not the same as executable. A sentence

[1] 1 `https://unifiedprocess.ai`

S. Martinelli, *Spec-Driven Development*, Apress Pocket Guides,
https://doi.org/10.1007/979-8-8688-2851-5_4

may sound clear and still leave crucial decisions unstated. Spec-driven development raises the quality bar: a specification must be precise enough to drive action, not just understandable enough to read.

This chapter explains how to write such specifications in practice.

What Executable Really Means

Executable does not mean formal notation, generated code, or machine-only syntax. It does not require a specialized modeling language. In many projects, plain Markdown is enough.

Executable means that the behavior described in the specification can be implemented, tested, and reviewed without hidden interpretation. Figure 4-1 compares a readable and an executable specification.

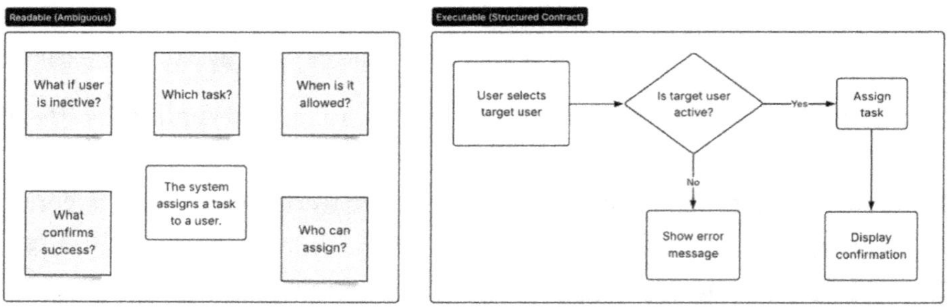

***Figure 4-1.** Readable vs. Executable*

Three simple tests reveal whether a use case is executable:

- If two people read it and imagine different outcomes, it is not executable yet.
- If a tester cannot derive acceptance criteria from it, it is not executable yet.
- If an AI tool must invent missing rules to generate code, it is not executable yet.

Consider the sentence: "The system assigns a task to a user." It is readable, but it leaves too many questions unanswered.

- Who is allowed to assign the task? Can a task be reassigned?
- Must the target user be active?
- What happens if the task does not exist?
- What outcome is guaranteed after success, and what remains unchanged after failure?

An executable version answers these questions explicitly through preconditions, a main flow, possible alternatives, and a guaranteed outcome. The core idea is simple: a good specification removes assumptions instead of depending on them.

Observable Behavior As the Core Principle

The most important discipline in writing system use cases is focusing on observable behavior: what an actor does and how the system responds in ways that can be seen, verified, or tested from the outside.

A use case should describe behavior such as

- The actor selects a task
- The system displays the task details
- The actor chooses a target user
- The system confirms the assignment

It should not describe internal implementation details such as

- The database transaction is opened
- A repository method is called
- A message is published internally
- The UI framework refreshes a component tree

These internal details may matter during design and implementation, but they do not belong to the executable contract. They are too unstable: architecture changes, frameworks change, internal components get replaced. The use case should remain valid even when the technical solution evolves. Figure 4-2 demonstrates this: the top shows observable behavior, while the bottom shows internal implementation.

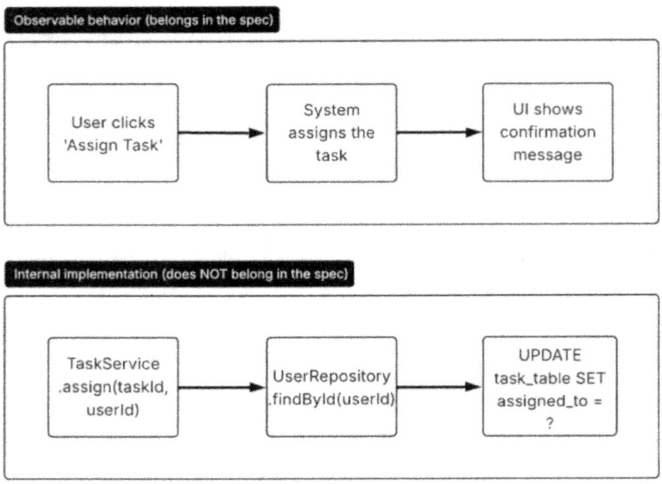

Figure 4-2. *Observable vs. Internal*

This matters even more over time. In long-running systems, code gets refactored, regenerated, modularized, or migrated. Observable behavior should remain stable across those changes. Specifications protect that stability by describing what the system does, not how it does it. A practical test: if a statement cannot be verified by observing the system from the outside, it probably does not belong in the use case.

Making Specifications Unambiguous

Ambiguity is the biggest risk in spec-driven development. AI does not create ambiguity, but it amplifies it: when a requirement or use case is vague, AI will still generate something that looks plausible and well structured, but that is based on interpretation rather than intent.

Words such as "normally," "quickly," "usually," "if possible," "as needed," and sometimes even "should" often hide decisions that have not yet been made. Consider the statement: "The system normally assigns the task." What counts as normal? In which cases does assignment not happen? Is the exception technical, business-related, or permission-related? Who decides?

An executable specification replaces vague wording with explicit rules. Instead of saying that the system responds quickly, it references a measurable non-functional requirement. Instead of saying that a user can assign tasks, it defines under which conditions assignment is allowed and what happens when those conditions are not met. Instead of saying that invalid input is handled appropriately, it states the observable result, such as an error message being shown and no change being persisted. Specificity is what makes a specification strong, not abstraction.

A concrete example shows the difference. Consider a simple statement from an early draft of a use case:

"The system should normally allow a user to assign a task to another user quickly, and handle invalid input appropriately."

This sentence is readable, but it is not executable. It hides at least four open decisions. When does "normally" not apply? How fast is "quickly"? Who counts as "another user"? What does "appropriately" mean when input is invalid?

The executable version makes each rule explicit:

Precondition: The acting user is authenticated and has the role *Team Member*.

Main flow:

1. The user selects a task with status `OPEN`.
2. The user selects a target user from the list of active team members.
3. The system assigns the task to the target user and sets the status to `ASSIGNED`.
4. The system shows a confirmation message and notifies the target user.

Alternative flow A1 (target user is inactive):

1. The system does not assign the task.
2. The system shows the message "The selected user is not active and cannot receive tasks."

Business rules:

- BR-012: A task can only be assigned if its status is `OPEN`.
- BR-013: A task can only be assigned to a user whose `active` flag is `true`.

Linked non-functional requirement:

- NFR-001: Task operations must complete in under one second.

Postconditions (success):

- The task has status `ASSIGNED`.
- The task references the target user.
- The target user has received a notification.

Compare both versions. The first sentence could be implemented in many different ways, all of them defensible. The second version leaves no room for interpretation. Two developers reading it will arrive at the same understanding. An AI agent generating code will produce predictable results. A tester can derive concrete test cases directly from the flow, the alternative, and the postconditions.

This is what executable means in practice. The specification does not describe the behavior in general terms. It defines the behavior in a way that can be observed, verified, and tested.

One Rule per Statement

When a sentence contains multiple decisions, it becomes harder to validate and easier to misunderstand. A sentence with "and" or "or" often hides separate rules that should be written independently.

For example: "The system validates the user and assigns the task." This combines at least two behaviors. Validation and assignment are not the same thing. They may fail for different reasons, trigger different messages, and lead to different test cases. Splitting them produces a clearer result:

1. The system validates that the selected target user is active.
2. The system assigns the task to the selected user.

This small change improves readability, testability, and maintainability. It also matters for long-term evolution: when rules are written in smaller, explicit units, later changes produce smaller diffs that are easier to review and easier to synchronize into code and tests. Specifications are not static documents; they evolve, and smaller units make that evolution manageable.

System Use Cases As Executable Contracts

In the AI Unified Process, system use cases are the main executable specification artifact. Requirements explain why something matters. The entity model defines the shared language of the domain. System use cases describe how the system behaves to fulfill a goal, which is why they sit at the center of the process.

A system use case defines one meaningful interaction between an actor and the system. It describes the starting point, the normal success path, relevant alternatives, and the guaranteed outcome, turning stakeholder intent into an explicit behavioral contract. Because the use case describes observable behavior, it can be understood by different roles without requiring them to think in code. Business stakeholders can validate that the behavior matches their expectations. Developers can derive implementation tasks. Testers can derive acceptance criteria. AI tools can work from a stable contract instead of guessing what the user probably meant.

Chapter 3 already introduced the structure of a system use case. The focus here is on how to write each part so that it becomes executable rather than merely descriptive.

Writing the Use Case Overview Well

The overview gives the use case its identity and intent. The use case ID creates stable traceability. The name should describe the goal clearly and specifically. The primary actor should identify who initiates the interaction. The goal should describe the successful outcome from the actor's perspective.

A common weakness is that goals are written as actions instead of outcomes. "Assign task" names an action. "Assign a task to another active user" describes a successful result, and it already hints at an important business condition: the target user must be active. The overview should orient the reader quickly without trying to explain the whole flow; that is the purpose of the main scenario and the alternative flows.

Writing Good Preconditions

Preconditions define what must already be true before the use case can begin. They are assumptions that define the starting line, not validations inside the flow.

For example:

- The actor is authenticated.
- The task exists.
- The task is currently unassigned.

These statements clarify the context in which the use case is valid. If one of them is not true, the use case does not start in the form described: either another use case applies, or an alternative business flow must be specified.

Teams often misuse preconditions in one of two ways: they leave them out completely, creating hidden assumptions, or they put ordinary validation logic there, making the flow incomplete. A good precondition answers a single question: what must already be true before the first step of the described interaction can happen?

Writing a Strong Main Success Scenario

The main success scenario describes the normal successful path from the actor's first action to the successful outcome. It is a sequence of observable steps, not a narrative summary. Each step should be ordered, externally visible, written in active language, and focused on one behavior.

Alternating between actor actions and system responses gives the scenario a natural rhythm that is easy to follow:

1. The actor opens the task details.
2. The system displays the task details and a list of active users.
3. The actor selects a target user.
4. The system validates that the selected user is active.
5. The system assigns the task to the selected user.
6. The system confirms the assignment.

Every step here can be understood and verified from the outside. A weak main flow typically contains technical details, skips important decisions, combines multiple rules into one step, uses vague wording like "processes the request," or ends without a clearly visible outcome. A well-written main flow is concrete enough that a tester could already sketch the corresponding test cases.

To make this concrete, consider how the same use case might look in a weak first draft:

1. The user opens the assignment screen.
2. The system processes the request and loads the necessary data.
3. The user picks someone and submits the form.
4. The system validates the input, checks permissions, applies business rules, and updates the database.
5. The task is assigned successfully.

At first glance, this looks reasonable. It reads like a description of what happens. But it fails several executability checks.

Step 2 is not observable. "Processes the request" describes internal work, not behavior that can be seen or verified from the outside. A tester cannot write an assertion against it.

Step 3 hides a decision. "Picks someone" leaves open which users are selectable, whether inactive users appear in the list, and what the system shows during selection.

Step 4 combines four independent rules into one step. Validation, permission checks, business rules, and persistence are different concerns. When any of them changes, it is unclear which step must be updated. Alternative and exception flows cannot reference a precise step number, because the step covers too much.

Step 5 ends with a passive statement. "The task is assigned successfully" describes a result, but not how the actor knows it. There is no confirmation message, no state change visible to the user, and no notification.

The recommended version shown earlier solves these problems. Each step is observable. Each step describes one behavior. Actor and system alternate clearly. The outcome is visible to the user, not just true in the database.

The difference is not stylistic. A weak main flow makes alternative flows harder to write, makes tests harder to derive, and gives AI agents too much room for interpretation. A strong main flow defines a stable contract that survives changes in implementation.

Writing Useful Alternative Flows

Alternative flows describe expected deviations from the main success scenario. They are not random edge cases but meaningful business variations that must be handled deliberately. If the selected target user is inactive, that is not a technical failure; it is a business-relevant alternative that should be visible in the specification.

Each alternative flow should begin with a clear trigger tied to a specific step in the main success scenario, so the reader knows exactly where the deviation occurs.

Example:

A1. Selected user is inactive

Trigger: At step 4, the selected user is inactive. Flow:

1. The system informs the actor that the selected user cannot receive tasks.
2. The system does not assign the task.
3. The use case ends without changes to the task assignment.

This is much stronger than writing "error is shown" because it makes the condition, the response, and the final state explicit.

A common mistake is to mix business alternatives and technical failures into the same category. They should be kept distinct. An inactive user, a missing permission, or an already completed task are business-related alternatives. A database outage or a network timeout belongs to technical handling and should not dominate the business use case. The use case defines expected system behavior from the business perspective.

Writing Clear Postconditions

Postconditions define what is guaranteed after the use case finishes, and they matter because they anchor the result. Without them, a flow may look plausible while the actual outcome remains unclear.

Success postconditions state what must be true after successful completion. Postconditions that represent a failure case state what is guaranteed to remain true if the use case is not complete successfully. For the assignment example:

Success:

- The task is assigned to the selected active user.

Failure:

- The task assignment remains unchanged.

These statements improve testing directly: a good test does not only check that a message was shown, it checks whether the final state matches the postconditions. If postconditions feel hard to write, that usually signals that the use case is still underspecified.

Writing Explicit Business Rules

Business rules should be visible and reusable, not buried inside prose. A business rule becomes more useful when it has its own identifier and clear wording, making it easier to reference from multiple use cases, tests, or review discussions.

For example:

- **BR-001:** Only active users can receive task assignments.
- **BR-002:** A completed task cannot be reassigned.

These rules are short, precise, and independent. Hidden rules are a common source of defects: a use case may look complete, but if key constraints live only in a sentence deep inside a paragraph, they are easily overlooked by both humans and AI. A good question to ask during review is: if this rule matters, can I point to it directly? If not, it needs to become an explicit rule.

From Use Cases to Acceptance Criteria

Acceptance criteria are not invented separately from use cases; they are derived from them. The main success scenario produces happy-path criteria. Alternative flows produce scenario-specific criteria. Business rules produce rule-level assertions. Postconditions produce final-state checks.

This derivation keeps tests aligned with intent. The use case defines the contract; acceptance criteria verify compliance with that contract, and automated tests become executable versions of those criteria. This also prevents a common problem in agile teams: requirements, acceptance criteria, and tests drifting apart because each is written independently. In the AI Unified Process, they are connected by design, and a well-written use case already contains the material from which acceptance criteria can be produced with little interpretation.

Just Enough Specification, Not Big Design Up Front

One of the biggest misunderstandings about executable specifications is the idea that they must be exhaustive. The AI Unified Process follows the principle of just enough specification: a specification should be precise enough for the next correct step, but no larger than necessary.

Teams often react to ambiguity by trying to define everything at once. They anticipate future features, rare edge cases, possible integrations, reporting needs, permission models, export scenarios, and operational concerns before the first clear use case is even finished. The result is not better clarity but a document full of speculation.

Consider a team building task assignment for a simple task manager. An over-specified early draft might try to cover all of these at once:

- Assignment to one or many users
- Immediate or scheduled assignment

- Delegation chains
- Temporary assignment expiration
- Workload-based assignment suggestions
- Reassignment notifications
- Audit export
- Permission models for team leads and administrators

All of these may become relevant later. But if the current requirement is simply that one user should be able to assign an open task to another active user, most of that detail is premature. A just-enough specification focuses on the current business need:

Use Case ID: UC-001
Use Case Name: Assign Task
Primary Actor: User
Goal: Assign an open task to another active user
Preconditions:

- The actor is authenticated.
- The task exists.
- The task is open.

Main Success Scenario:

1. The actor opens the task details.
2. The system displays the task details and available active users.
3. The actor selects a target user.
4. The system validates that the selected user is active.
5. The system assigns the task to the selected user.
6. The system confirms the assignment.

Alternative Flows

A1: Selected user is inactive

Trigger: At step 4, the selected user is inactive.

Flow:

1. The system informs the actor that the selected user cannot receive tasks.
2. The system does not assign the task.

Postconditions:

Success:

- The task is assigned to the selected active user.

Failure:

- The task assignment remains unchanged.

Business Rules:

- Only active users can receive task assignments.
- Completed tasks cannot be assigned.

This is enough for implementation and testing. It is precise, reviewable, and bounded. It does not guess future delegation rules, bulk assignment, or scheduling behavior. If those needs become real later, they should appear as new requirements and new or extended use cases.

Just enough does not mean vague. It means disciplined: being explicit about today's behavior and refusing to speculate about tomorrow's. A useful signal is whether the team can already derive acceptance criteria. If they cannot, the use case is probably still unclear, and the correct response is to refine the specification rather than to start guessing.

Executable Specifications and AI

Executable specifications are especially powerful in the AI era because they provide boundaries. AI is strong at transformation: it can draft code, tests, migrations, UI structures, and documentation quickly. But it struggles with missing intent. When a specification leaves important questions unanswered, AI fills the gap with plausible assumptions that may look reasonable but do not match what was actually intended.

This means that clarity matters more now, not less. Executable specifications reduce hallucination by removing ambiguity. They improve consistency because all generated artifacts derive from the same contract. They make review easier because humans can compare code and tests against a stable behavioral reference. The practical shift is this: instead of asking AI to invent behavior, you ask it to implement clearly defined behavior. That turns AI from a guessing collaborator into a bounded execution partner.

Key Takeaways

Executable specifications describe observable system behavior with enough precision that implementation and verification can follow without guesswork. Their purpose is to remove interpretation, not to sound formal.

System use cases are the central executable artifact because they turn stakeholder intent into explicit behavioral contracts. Writing them well requires care at every level: goals should describe outcomes, preconditions should define the starting line, flows should contain ordered observable steps, alternative flows should make deviations explicit, postconditions should anchor the outcome, and business rules should be visible and reusable.

The principle of just enough specification protects teams from big design up front. A good specification defines the current behavior clearly enough to implement, test, review, and evolve. It does not try to capture every possible future variation. This discipline becomes even more important when AI is involved: clear executable specifications create the boundaries that make AI output more reliable, more predictable, and easier to validate.

The next chapter shows how these executable specifications begin to drive code directly.

CHAPTER 5

Specs Driving Code in Practice

The previous chapters introduced the specification artifacts of the AI Unified Process: requirements that capture intent, an entity model that gives the team a shared vocabulary, and system use cases that describe observable behavior from the user's point of view.

At that point, the specification is clear, reviewable, and versioned. But one important question remains: What happens next?

A specification has value only if it changes how development happens. If a team writes good use cases but then returns to ad hoc prompting, the specification becomes passive documentation again. The agent works from the latest prompt, not from the approved artifact. Two weeks later, code and specification disagree, and nobody is sure which one is right.

This chapter closes that gap. It shows how a system use case becomes the entry point for daily development work. We will follow one example through the complete workflow: first implementation, review, later change, and synchronization.

The example is UC-012 Assign Task. It is small enough to understand quickly but realistic enough to show the important parts of the process.

The goal of this chapter is not to explain every tool in detail. That comes later. The goal is to show the execution model: a system use case becomes the input for an AI agent, the agent applies project guidelines and technical knowledge, and the result is reviewed as a normal code change.

S. Martinelli, *Spec-Driven Development*, Apress Pocket Guides,
https://doi.org/10.1007/979-8-8688-2851-5_5

From Passive Specs to Active Specs

A passive specification describes the system, but it does not drive the work. It may be written well. It may even be stored in Git. But if developers ignore it when changing the system, it becomes just another document.

An active specification is different. It is the starting point for implementation. It defines what needs to change before code is touched. The developer does not ask the AI agent to "add some validation" or "build a form." The developer asks the agent to implement or synchronize a specific use case.

This changes the nature of the instruction.

Instead of this:

```
Add validation to the task assignment form.
```

the instruction becomes this:

```
Implement UC-012.
```

or later:

```
Synchronize the implementation with the updated UC-012.
```

The difference is important. The first prompt is open-ended. The agent must guess the scope, the terminology, the rules, and the expected outcome. The second instruction points to an approved behavioral contract. The agent reads the use case and works within its boundaries.

That is the practical meaning of spec-driven development. The specification is not only a description. It is the control point for change.

The Running Example: UC-012 Assign Task

Assume that the team has already written and reviewed the following system use case.

```
Use Case ID: UC-012
Use Case Name: Assign Task
Primary Actor: User
Goal: Assign an open task to another active user
Status: Approved

Linked Requirements:
- FR-004 Assign task to user
- NFR-002 Task operations complete within one second
- C-001 Backend uses Java and PostgreSQL

Preconditions:
- The user is authenticated.
- The task exists.
- The task is open and not yet assigned.

Main Success Scenario:
1. User opens the task details.
2. System displays the task and a list of active users.
3. User selects a target user.
4. User confirms the assignment.
5. System validates that the target user is active.
6. System assigns the task to the selected user.
7. System confirms that the task was assigned.

Alternative Flow A1: Target user is inactive
Trigger:
- The selected target user is inactive.

Flow:
- System rejects the assignment.
- System shows that only active users can receive tasks.
- Task remains unchanged.
```

```
Postconditions:
Success:
- Task is assigned to the selected active user.
- Task status is ASSIGNED.

Failure:
- Task remains unchanged.

Business Rules:
BR-012-1: Only active users can receive tasks.
BR-012-2: An assigned task must have exactly one assignee.
```

This use case is the source of truth for the change. It defines the actor, the goal, the preconditions, the main flow, the alternative flow, the postconditions, and the business rules.

The use case does not describe the database schema. It does not mention Vaadin components, service classes, SQL queries, or controller methods. Those are implementation concerns. The use case describes observable behavior. That is what makes it stable enough to drive code.

What the Agent Reads Before Writing Code

When the developer asks the agent to implement `UC-012`, the agent does not work from the use case alone. It reads the use case as the main input, but it also needs the surrounding project context.

In a typical repository, the relevant files are

```
/docs/requirements.md
/docs/entity-model.md
/docs/use-cases/UC-012-assign-task.md
CLAUDE.md or AGENTS.md
src/main
src/test
```

The use case defines the behavior. The requirements explain the intent and constraints. The entity model defines the domain terms. The guideline file defines project rules that apply to every agent interaction. The existing source code and tests show the current implementation structure.

This combination is important. Without the use case, the agent does not know what behavior to implement. Without the entity model, it may use inconsistent terminology. Without the guideline file, it may ignore project conventions. Without the existing code, it may generate something that does not fit the application.

The agent therefore works from a bounded context, not from an isolated prompt.

Implementing the Use Case for the First Time

Once the use case has been reviewed and approved, the developer can ask the agent to implement it.

In a command-based workflow, this could look like this:

```
/implement UC-012
```

The exact command name is not important. What matters is the structure of the request. The agent is not asked to invent a feature. It is asked to implement a specific use case.

The workflow looks like in Figure 5-1.

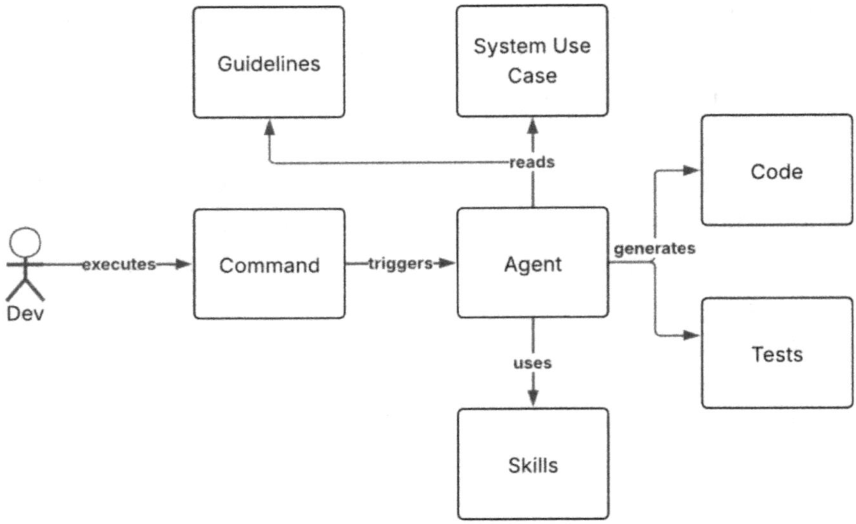

Figure 5-1. *Workflow*

For the Assign Task use case, the implementation may involve several parts of the system:

- A Vaadin view that displays the task details and target users
- An application service that performs the assignment
- A jOOQ query that loads assignable users
- Validation logic that rejects inactive users
- Tests that verify the main flow and alternative flow

The important point is not which files are changed. The important point is why they are changed. Each change must trace back to the use case.

If the generated code adds behavior that is not described in UC-012, that is a problem. If the generated code misses a business rule from UC-012, that is also a problem. The use case is the reference for review.

How Use Case Elements Map to Code

A system use case is structured in a way that naturally maps to implementation concerns.

For `UC-012`, the mapping could look like this:

Use case element	Implementation consequence
Preconditions	Check that the task exists, is open, and is not already assigned
Main flow step 2	Display task details and active users
Main flow step 5	Validate that the selected user is active
Main flow step 6	Assign the task in the application service
Alternative Flow A1	Reject inactive users and show a clear message
Success postcondition	Persist assignee and set task status to ASSIGNED
Failure postcondition	Leave the task unchanged
BR-012-1	Add validation rule for active users
BR-012-2	Ensure exactly one assignee

This mapping keeps the implementation grounded. The agent can derive code structure from the use case without guessing the behavior.

It also makes review easier. The reviewer can compare the generated diff against the use case section by section. Does the code check the preconditions? Does the UI support the main flow? Does the service enforce the business rules? Does the failure path leave the task unchanged?

The review is no longer a general opinion about generated code. It is a comparison against the behavioral contract.

Guideline Files As Project Memory

The use case defines what the system must do. But the agent also needs to know how this project is built.

That information belongs in a guideline file such as `CLAUDE.md` or `AGENTS.md` at the root of the repository.

For the example stack used in this book, such a file might contain rules like this:

```
# Project Guidelines

- Use Java, Spring Boot, Vaadin, jOOQ, and PostgreSQL.
- Implement business logic in application services.
- Do not put SQL queries into Vaadin views.
- Use jOOQ for database access.
- Keep Vaadin views thin.
- Reference the use case ID in generated tests.
- Do not regenerate existing code when synchronizing a use case.
- Keep changes scoped to the requested use case.
```

These rules are not part of `UC-012` because they are not specific to task assignment. They apply across the project.

Guideline files act as executable project memory. They give the agent stable rules that should be respected on every task. This prevents the same architectural decisions from being repeated in every prompt.

The file should stay short. If it becomes too large, the agent has to process too much information on every request. Long guideline files also become harder to review and maintain. Rules that apply only to one specific workflow should live in a skill or task-specific instruction, not in the global guideline file.

Because guideline files are stored in Git, changes to them are visible. If the team changes an architectural rule, that change is reviewed like any other important project change.

Skills and Plugins As Repeatable Workflows

The command `/implement UC-012` is not just a nicer prompt. It represents a repeatable workflow.

Behind the command is a skill. A skill is a reusable capability that tells the agent how to perform a specific kind of work. For example:

- Expand a requirement into a system use case
- Implement a use case
- Generate a Flyway migration from an entity model change
- Derive Karibu tests from use case flows
- Create Playwright tests for an end-to-end scenario

A skill gives structure to AI interaction. It defines what the agent should read, what it should produce, and what constraints it should respect.

Plugins make this stack-specific. The AI Unified Process itself does not depend on Java, Vaadin, jOOQ, or Spring Boot. Those are implementation choices. A stack plugin connects the general process to a concrete technology stack.

For the example in this book, a Vaadin and jOOQ plugin might know how to

- Create a Vaadin view from a use case
- Generate jOOQ queries for the entity model
- Write application services according to the project structure
- Generate Karibu tests for Vaadin views
- Generate Playwright tests for full system behavior

Another team could use the same process with a different plugin for a different stack. The methodology remains stable. The execution layer changes.

This separation matters because specifications should outlive frameworks and tools. A system use case written today should still be useful if the team changes the UI framework later. The implementation plugin may change, but the behavior remains defined in the specification.

MCP Servers for Technical Accuracy

A specification defines what the system must do. It does not define every detail of a framework API.

For example, `UC-012` says that the system displays task details and a list of active users. It does not explain how to configure a Vaadin Grid, how to bind a ComboBox, or how to write a jOOQ query.

This is where technical context becomes important.

Modern AI agents often know many frameworks, but their knowledge may be incomplete or outdated. APIs change. Best practices change. Components evolve. If the agent relies only on training data, it may generate code that looks plausible but does not match the current library version.

Model Context Protocol servers, or MCP servers, address this problem by giving the agent access to structured technical documentation and tools at generation time.

In the `UC-012` example

- The specification tells the agent that active users must be displayed.
- The Vaadin documentation tells the agent how to implement the UI correctly.
- The jOOQ documentation tells the agent how to write the query correctly.
- The project guideline file tells the agent where the code belongs.

These inputs complement each other.

```
Specification = what the system must do
Guidelines = how this project is structured
MCP = how the current technical API works
```

This reduces hallucination. The agent does not need to guess how the current Vaadin or jOOQ API works. It can query the relevant technical context.

MCP does not replace specifications. It supports implementation. The specification remains the source of truth for behavior.

Version Control As the Safety Net

All specification artifacts, guideline files, code, and tests live in the same repository. This is essential.

A typical implementation of `UC-012` happens on a branch. The pull request contains the use case and all generated or modified code. This makes the change reviewable as one unit.

The pull request should show

```
/docs/use-cases/UC-012-assign-task.md
src/main/...
src/test/...
```

The reviewer starts with the specification. Is the behavior correct? Are the rules explicit? Are the postconditions clear? Are the alternative flows complete enough?

Only after that does the reviewer inspect the implementation. This order matters. If the team reviews the code first, it may accidentally approve an implementation before agreeing on what the behavior should be.

The correct review order is

1. Review the specification.
2. Confirm the behavior is correct.
3. Review the implementation.
4. Check that the code matches the specification.
5. Check that tests cover the specified flows and rules.

Version control also makes AI-generated work safe. If the generated result is wrong, the branch can be discarded. The cost of a bad generation is limited. Nothing enters the main branch without review.

Synchronizing Code When a Use Case Changes

The first implementation is only the beginning. Most real software work happens later when behavior changes.

Assume the business changes the assignment rule. Originally, `UC-012` allowed only active users to receive tasks.

The old business rule was

```
BR-012-1: Only active users can receive tasks.
```

Later, the business decides that team leads may assign tasks to inactive users in special cases.

The use case is updated first:

```
BR-012-1: Active users can receive tasks.
BR-012-2: Inactive users can receive tasks only if the
assigning user has the Team Lead role.
```

The alternative flow is also updated:

```
Alternative Flow A1: Target user is inactive and assigner is
not Team Lead
```

```
Trigger:
- The selected target user is inactive.
- The assigning user does not have the Team Lead role.

Flow:
- System rejects the assignment.
- System shows that inactive users can only receive tasks from
  a Team Lead.
- Task remains unchanged.

Alternative Flow A2: Target user is inactive and assigner is
Team Lead
Trigger:
- The selected target user is inactive.
- The assigning user has the Team Lead role.

Flow:
- System allows the assignment.
- System records that the assignment was made by a Team Lead.
- System confirms that the task was assigned.
```

Only after this specification change has been made and reviewed should the implementation change.

The developer now asks the agent to synchronize the code:

```
/implement UC-012
```

Synchronization is different from regeneration.

Regeneration means creating the implementation again from scratch. That usually produces large diffs. Existing structure may be rewritten. Custom refactorings may be lost. Review becomes difficult because the diff contains too many unrelated changes.

Synchronization means applying only the behavioral change described by the updated use case.

The agent compares the previous and current version of `UC-012`. It sees that the assignment rule has changed. It then updates the affected parts of the code:

- Validation logic
- Role check
- UI feedback message
- Tests for inactive users
- Possibly audit logging if required by the updated postconditions

Everything else should remain unchanged.

This is one of the most important practical benefits of spec-driven development. The specification change creates a small, reviewable implementation change.

Regeneration vs. Synchronization

The difference between regeneration and synchronization is worth making explicit.

Situation	Better approach	Reason
New use case without existing implementation	Generate	There is no existing code to preserve
Small behavior change in existing use case	Synchronize	Only the affected behavior should change
Entity model extended with one field	Synchronize	Existing structure should remain stable

(continued)

Situation	Better approach	Reason
Prototype thrown away	Regenerate	Long-term preservation does not matter
Existing production feature modified	Synchronize	Reviewability and safety matter
Major architectural reset	Regenerate with care	This is a deliberate migration, not a normal change

In long-living systems, synchronization is usually the safer default. It protects existing design decisions and keeps diffs small.

This is especially important when AI is involved. AI can produce a lot of code very quickly. Without synchronization discipline, a small behavior change may become a large rewrite. That makes review harder and increases the risk of accidental drift.

Tests Follow the Same Use Case

Although the next chapter focuses on testing, it is important to mention the connection here.

When `UC-012` is implemented, tests should be derived from the same use case. The main success scenario becomes the happy-path test. Alternative flows become additional test scenarios. Business rules become assertions.

For the first version of `UC-012`, the tests may include

- Assigning an open task to an active user succeeds
- Assigning a task to an inactive user fails
- Failed assignment leaves the task unchanged
- Successful assignment changes the task status to `ASSIGNED`

After the rule changes, the tests change as well:

- Assigning an inactive user as a normal user fails
- Assigning an inactive user as a Team Lead succeeds
- Failed assignment still leaves the task unchanged
- Assignment by a Team Lead is recorded if the use case requires it

The tests are not invented independently. They are the verification view of the same behavioral contract.

This keeps code and tests aligned with the specification. It also gives the team regression protection when other use cases change later.

Reviewing Specification and Code Together

Human review remains essential. AI can generate implementation code, update tests, and follow project rules. But it cannot take responsibility for business correctness.

The reviewer must check two things.

First, the specification must be correct. Does the use case describe the intended behavior? Are the rules explicit? Are the alternatives clear? Are the postconditions strong enough?

Second, the implementation must match the specification. The generated code should do what the use case says, no more and no less.

For `UC-012`, useful review questions are

- Does the code assign only tasks that are open and unassigned?
- Does it reject inactive users according to the current rule?
- Does it preserve the task when assignment fails?

- Does the UI show the correct feedback?
- Do tests cover the main success scenario and alternative flows?
- Does every meaningful change trace back to the use case?

This review style changes the conversation. Instead of asking whether the code "looks good," the reviewer asks whether the code fulfills the approved behavior.

That is a much stronger question.

Human Responsibility Does Not Disappear

Spec-driven development with AI does not remove developers from the process. It changes where their judgment matters most.

Developers and architects define the boundaries. They write and review specifications. They decide which behavior is correct. They define project rules. They review generated diffs. They ensure that the implementation remains understandable and maintainable.

AI helps with the mechanical translation from specification to code and tests. This is valuable because the translation work is often repetitive and error-prone. But the responsibility for meaning remains human.

The most important decisions move earlier in the process. They happen when the use case is written, reviewed, and approved. That is where ambiguity is cheapest to fix.

If the specification is wrong, AI will implement the wrong thing quickly. If the specification is clear, AI can help implement it consistently.

A Complete Change Flow

The complete flow for a new use case looks like in Figure 5-2.

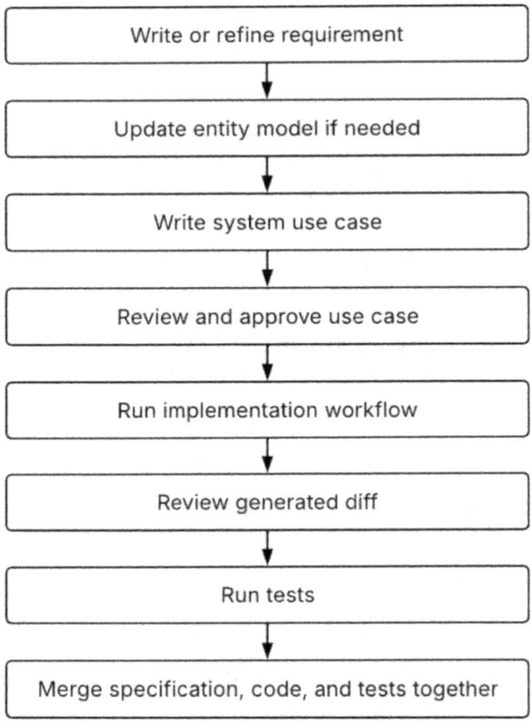

***Figure 5-2.** Complete Workflow*

For an existing use case, the flow is similar, but the focus is synchronization. That's what Figure 5-3 shows.

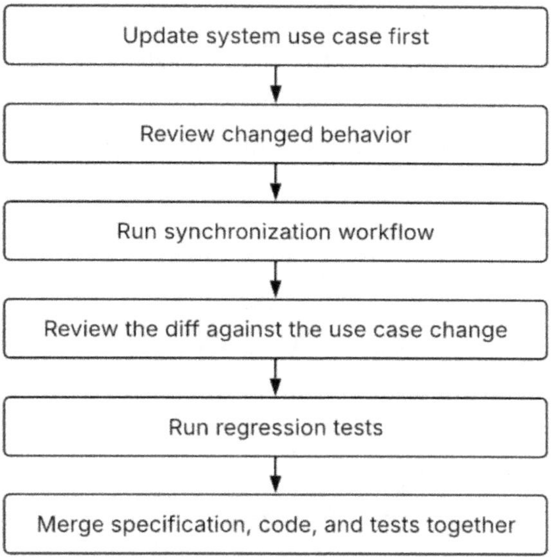

Figure 5-3. *Synchronization Workflow*

This is the daily rhythm of the AI Unified Process. The specification changes first. Code and tests follow. Review keeps the loop safe.

Key Takeaways

Specifications become valuable when they actively drive development. A system use case is not only documentation. It is the entry point for implementation and change.

In daily work, the developer does not ask an AI agent to make vague improvements. The developer references a specific use case, such as `UC-012`, and asks the agent to implement or synchronize that behavior.

The agent reads more than the use case. It also uses linked requirements, the entity model, project guideline files, existing code, and technical context from tools such as MCP servers. Together, these inputs give the agent a bounded and reliable working context.

Use case elements map naturally to code. Preconditions become checks. Main flow steps become the happy-path implementation. Alternative flows become branches and validation behavior. Postconditions define the expected outcome. Business rules become explicit logic and assertions.

Guideline files such as `CLAUDE.md` or `AGENTS.md` act as executable project memory. They define rules that apply across the project and help the agent behave consistently over time.

Skills and plugins make AI interaction repeatable. Skills define reusable workflows, while stack plugins adapt the process to a concrete technology stack. The methodology remains stable even when the implementation technology changes.

Synchronization is different from regeneration. New use cases may be generated from scratch, but existing behavior should usually be synchronized. This keeps diffs small, preserves existing design decisions, and makes review safer.

Version control is the safety net. Specifications, code, tests, and guideline files live in the same repository. Pull requests show behavioral changes and implementation changes together.

Human review remains essential. AI can translate clear specifications into code and tests, but it cannot decide whether the behavior is correct for the business. That responsibility stays with the team.

The next chapter applies the same principle to testing. The same system use cases that drive implementation also drive verification. Code is the implementation view of the use case. Tests are its verification view.

CHAPTER 6

Specs As Tests

In Chapter 5, specifications became operational. A system use case stopped being documentation and became the entry point for code generation and synchronization. Behavior first changed in the specification, then the code change followed. The same logic applies to tests.

In the AI Unified Process, tests are not a separate activity or a late-phase quality gate. They are another projection of the same behavioral contract. If code is the implementation view of a system use case, tests are its verification view. Both originate from the same artifact, and both evolve through the same synchronization process.

But tests also serve a second purpose: they are the guardrail that makes controlled evolution possible.

Why Testing Matters Even More in the AI Era

Generative AI dramatically increases the speed at which code can be produced. A new use case can be scaffolded in minutes, a synchronization step can touch dozens of files, and refactorings that once took days are now cheap. That speed is useful, but it also amplifies the cost of mistakes.

S. Martinelli, *Spec-Driven Development*, Apress Pocket Guides,
https://doi.org/10.1007/979-8-8688-2851-5_6

Without strong tests, rapid generation becomes fragile. A small specification change can silently break unrelated behavior. Synchronization can introduce regressions that are hard to trace. Refactoring can alter business rules in ways that only surface later in production.

Tests counterbalance that acceleration. In a spec-driven workflow, they serve three roles: they verify that the implementation fulfills the current specification, they catch unintended side effects when other use cases change, and they prevent drift between what the specification says and what the software actually does.

From Specification to Executable Guardrail

A system use case already contains everything you need to write tests. Preconditions describe the required setup. The main success scenario describes the happy path. Alternative flows describe valid variations. Exception flows describe error conditions. Postconditions describe the guarantees after a successful run. Business rules describe the constraints that apply throughout the use case.

Tests are not invented alongside specifications, they are derived from them. The mapping is straightforward: the main success scenario becomes the primary positive test, each alternative flow becomes its own scenario, each exception flow becomes a negative test, and business rules become explicit assertions.

Once implemented, these tests form a firewall around the behavior they cover (Figure 6-1).

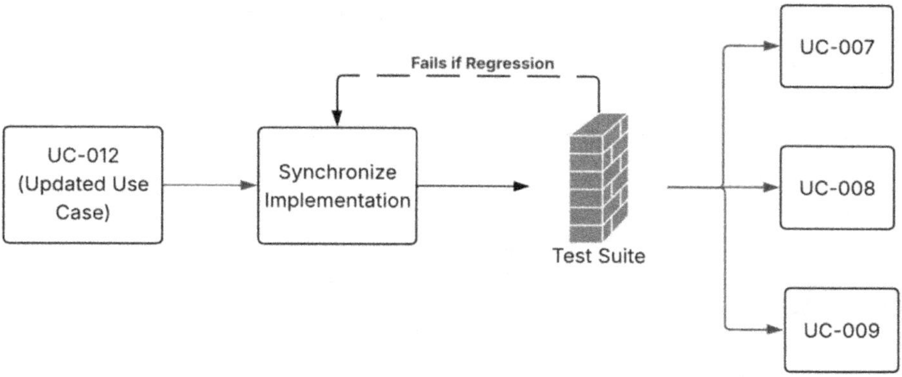

Figure 6-1. *Protected by Test Firewall*

Consider a system with ten implemented use cases, each with derived tests. When one use case changes, the specification is updated and the agent synchronizes implementation and the related tests. What protects the other nine? Their tests do. If the change to UC-012 accidentally breaks behavior defined in UC-007, that test fails immediately. This is not accidental safety; it is a structural property of the approach.

Regression Protection

Most systems are not built in one go. Business rules get clarified. Compliance requirements arrive. Edge cases appear. Performance constraints tighten. Each change is local in intent but potentially global in impact.

The key property of spec-driven tests is that they protect observable behavior, not internal structure. This distinction matters a lot in practice. If tests are tied to implementation details, every refactoring becomes painful because you have to rewrite the tests alongside the code. If tests are tied to specification-defined behavior, refactoring is safe, you can rearrange the internals freely as long as the observable results stay correct.

This is what makes synchronization viable over time. Without regression protection, you would have to regenerate rather than synchronize because you could never be confident that a targeted change had not broken something elsewhere. With it, change becomes deliberate rather than risky.

Test Layers and Strategy: The Test Trophy

A common model for organizing tests is the test pyramid, which suggests many unit tests at the base, fewer integration tests in the middle, and even fewer end-to-end tests at the top. This model was designed for traditional architectures with expensive browser-based UI tests.

For modern business applications with frameworks like Vaadin and Spring Boot, the pyramid does not tell the whole story. A more accurate model is the test trophy, introduced by Kent C. Dodds. The trophy, as shown in Figure 6-2, puts integration tests at the center, because they give the best return: they test real behavior with real infrastructure, without the cost of a browser.

> ***The Test Trophy:*** *Static analysis at the base, a small layer of unit tests for pure logic, a large layer of integration tests for services and repositories, and a smaller layer of end-to-end tests at the top. The wide middle is intentional.*

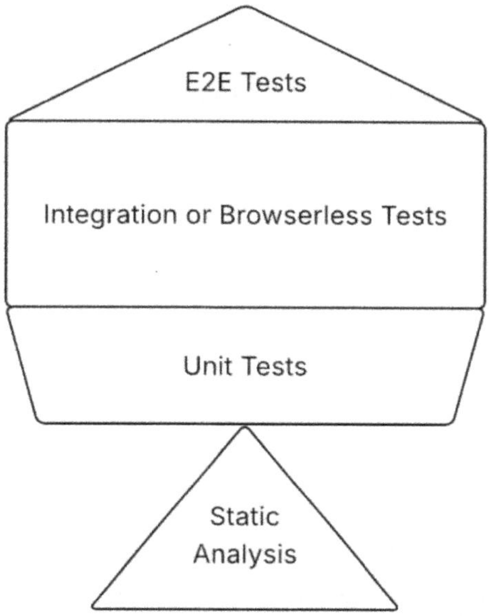

Figure 6-2. *Test Trophy*

This matches how business applications actually work. Most of the interesting behavior lives in services and database interactions, not in isolated functions or in the browser. Testing that layer thoroughly with real infrastructure gives you confidence without the fragility of full browser automation.

The test trophy also gives a clear decision rule for system use cases. If a use case has a UI, the primary test is a browserless test. It exercises the full flow from the view down to the database without a browser. If a use case has no UI, for example, a REST API or a background job, the primary test is an integration test. It invokes the service or endpoint directly and asserts on the result. The specification tells you which case applies. You do not need to think about it per test; you need to think about it per use case.

Static Analysis

At the base of the trophy sits static analysis. Tools like SonarQube, Checkstyle, FindBugs, NullAway, or ArchUnit catch problems before any test runs. In a Spring Boot project, ArchUnit can enforce architectural rules directly: for example, that services do not depend on the web layer, or that only repositories access the database. These checks are instant and require no infrastructure.

Unit Tests

Unit tests cover business logic in isolation. They are fast, have no infrastructure dependencies, and map directly to individual business rules and postconditions. A rule like “a task title must not be empty” is a unit test. So is “a discount above 30% requires manager approval.” These tests should be numerous, but they are not the main layer in the trophy.

Integration Tests

Integration tests are the core of the test trophy in a business application. They test application services and repositories against a real database. Testcontainers starts a database container for the test run. The test invokes a service method and asserts on the resulting database state or returned value.

This layer verifies that persistence, transactions, and constraint enforcement work together as the use case expects. One integration test per main success scenario is a reasonable baseline, with additional tests for exception flows that involve database constraints or validation.

```
@SpringBootTest
@Transactional
class TaskServiceIT {
```

```
    @Autowired
    TaskService taskService;

    @Test
    @UseCase(id = "UC-05", scenario = "Main")
    void assign_task_to_active_user_succeeds() {
        var task = taskService.assignTask(activeUserId,
        taskId);
        assertThat(task.getAssignee()).isEqualTo(activeUserId);
    }
}
```

End-to-End Tests: Two Approaches for Vaadin

End-to-end tests cover observable UI behavior. For Vaadin applications, two tools are practical, and they serve different purposes: Browserless Testing and Playwright.

Browserless Testing runs the Vaadin UI in a headless server-side simulation, without a browser. This is a key point: Browserless tests are not browser tests. They interact directly with the server-side component tree. This makes them fast, stable, and easy to run in any CI environment without display configuration.

Browserless tests sit in a special position in the trophy. They are end-to-end tests in the sense that they exercise a full use case from the UI layer down to the database, but they do not require a browser. They combine the coverage of E2E tests with the speed and reliability closer to integration tests.

```
class TaskViewTest extends BrowserlessTest {

    @Test
    @UseCase(id = "UC-05", scenario = "A1")
    void assign_to_inactive_user_shows_error() {
```

```
        UI.getCurrent().navigateTo(TaskView.class);

        var assign = _get(Button.class, spec -> spec.
        withText("Assign"));
        _click(assign);

expectNotifications("User is not active");
    }
}
```

Playwright drives a real browser and is the right choice when the test needs to verify rendered HTML output, CSS behavior, keyboard interaction, file downloads, or behavior that depends on the actual browser environment. Playwright tests are slower and require more infrastructure, so they should be used selectively for scenarios where the browser behavior itself is what you are testing.

Not every use case needs both. A use case with no meaningful browser-specific behavior doesn't need a Playwright test. The specification tells you which layers apply.

> ***Browserless vs. Playwright:*** *Use Browserless Testing for navigation, form validation, component state, and full use case flows without a browser. Use Playwright for rendered output, CSS, file handling, and browser-specific interactions.*

Trophy Overview

Table 6-1 summarizes the five layers and their key characteristics. The wide middle, integration tests and browserless tests is where most use cases are covered. Static analysis and unit tests form the cheap and fast foundation. Playwright sits at the top and is used selectively, only when the browser itself is relevant to the test.

Table 6-1. *Test Layers*

Layer	Speed	Browser	Scope	Quantity
Static analysis	Instant	No	Code rules	All code
Unit tests	Fast	No	Business logic	Many
Integration tests	Medium	No	Services + DB	Most (per use case)
Browserless Testing	Medium	No	Full UI flow	Most (per use case)
Playwright	Slow	Yes	Browser behavior	Selective

Where Test-Driven Development Fits

A reasonable question at this point is whether Test-Driven Development (TDD) still has a role if specifications come first. It does, but not as the primary organizing principle.

In an AI Unified Process workflow, the system use case still comes first. It defines the behavior that must exist. TDD then becomes a local design technique inside that larger specification-driven process. The sequence is therefore clear: first clarify and update the use case, then decide where test-first design helps, then implement. The specification defines what must happen. TDD helps shape how a particular rule, service, or API is realized in code.

Business logic is where TDD fits most naturally. Business rules are typically deterministic, independent of UI concerns, expressible as preconditions and postconditions, and easy to verify in isolation. The classic red-green-refactor cycle works extremely well here: write a failing test that encodes one business rule, implement the minimal logic to satisfy it, then refactor while keeping tests green. Each test maps directly to a rule or postcondition in the use case, and each becomes part of the growing guardrail.

Application services and APIs also benefit from a test-first approach. For a service, you can write a test that defines the accepted input, expected output, validation behavior, and relevant side effects before the internal structure exists. For an API endpoint, a test defines how it behaves from the outside, which requests it accepts, how input is validated, which responses and status codes it returns, how errors are represented, before any controller logic is written. In both cases, the test expresses the behavioral contract that comes from the use case. The implementation then follows that contract, and traceability to the use case ID is preserved.

User interfaces are different. A UI test must assume that concrete components exist, that layout decisions have been made, that interaction points are defined. Before the UI exists, there is nothing meaningful to test against, and trying to write tests first usually leads to fragile stubs that need to be rewritten as the UI stabilizes. This is not a failure of discipline; it is a mismatch between the technique and the layer. For UI behavior the sensible sequence is: specify the observable behavior, implement the UI, then write the tests. The point is not to apply TDD uniformly but to apply it where it fits the nature of what you are building.

Test Generation Workflow with AI

The mechanical part of deriving tests from a use case is well-suited to AI. The use case already contains the flows, business rules, preconditions, and postconditions. From that, an agent can generate a first test skeleton quickly. What matters is not the speed of generation, but the quality of review afterward.

For service and repository tests, I typically ask the agent to generate JUnit 5 tests with Spring Boot and Testcontainers, with one test method per flow and one per business rule. The generated methods should be named after the flow or rule they cover, reference the use case ID through annotations, use postconditions as assertions, and avoid checking internal implementation details.

For Vaadin UI tests, the AI Unified Process marketplace provides a /browserless-test slash command. It takes a use case and the relevant view class as input and generates Browserless Testing skeletons for the observable UI behavior described in the flows. This keeps the generated tests aligned with the conventions used in the rest of the suite.

The agent returns test classes for both layers. Before accepting them, review each test method against three questions:

1. Does the assertion match the postcondition in the use case?
2. Does the setup reflect only the stated preconditions?
3. Does the test really fail when the rule is violated?

Question three requires running the test against a deliberately broken implementation. If removing a validation check does not make the test fail, the test is not guarding that rule.

When a use case changes, the same prompts work for updates. Pass the diff of the use case and the existing test classes. The agent proposes additions and modifications. Apply the same three-question review to every changed method, not just the new ones. A small wording change in a business rule can produce a structurally identical test that asserts the wrong thing.

This keeps the generated tests aligned with the conventions used in the rest of the suite. The marketplace and its available commands are covered in Chapter 7.

Coverage As Specification Completeness

Traditional test coverage asks how many lines of code were executed. That question is useful, but it is not enough. Spec-driven coverage asks a more important question: which parts of the specification are actually verified?

The goal is complete specification coverage. Every main success scenario should have a corresponding happy-path test. Every alternative or exception flow should be covered where it matters. Every business rule should be asserted somewhere in the suite. An uncovered line of code may be acceptable. An uncovered business rule is a gap in the system's protection.

In my current projects, I make this traceability explicit in the test code itself. Test class names include the use case identifier and name, for example UC002CreateFormTest. Test methods point to the exact flow or business rule they verify, and in Java, I use dedicated annotations to capture these references in a structured way.

```
@Test
@UseCase(id = "UC-02", scenario = "A1")
void create_form_without_title_shows_validation_error() {
  ...
}
```

This shifts coverage reporting from code execution to specification verification. It makes visible which parts of the intended behavior are protected and which are still missing. Because those links are explicit, AI agents can also reason about gaps at the specification level, not just at the code level.

When Use Cases Change

The real value of spec-driven testing shows up when behavior evolves. Take a concrete example: a use case where only active users may be assigned tasks. Later, the business decides that administrators should be able to assign tasks to inactive users in special cases.

The change starts in the specification. The business rule is updated, an alternative flow is added, and the use case is reviewed and approved. Then synchronization runs: the implementation changes and the related tests are updated to match.

At that point the guardrails for the rest of the system activate. If the updated rule accidentally allows all users to assign tasks to inactive users, not just administrators, the business-rule tests for that scenario fail. If another use case relied implicitly on the old restriction, its tests fail. If the UI feedback is inconsistent with the new flow, the UI tests fail. Each failure points to a real alignment problem, not a false alarm.

Without derived tests, these regressions might go unnoticed until production. With them, they are caught during synchronization.

AI Generates Tests but Cannot Validate Them

AI can generate tests from specifications, update them when use cases change, and help detect missing coverage. That is valuable because keeping specifications and tests aligned becomes harder as a system grows.

What AI cannot do is judge whether a generated test reflects the intended behavior. A test may look plausible while still asserting the wrong postcondition, encoding a misunderstood business rule, or verifying something no stakeholder actually wanted.

That is why generated tests must always be reviewed by a human. Assertions need to be checked against the specification, business rules against stakeholder intent, and changed tests with the same care as newly generated ones. AI speeds up the mechanical work. Human review protects correctness.

Key Takeaways

Tests in the AI Unified Process are derived from system use cases. Main flows, alternative flows, exception flows, and business rules all map directly to executable checks. These tests protect observable behavior rather than implementation details. That is what makes refactoring and synchronization safe.

The right mental model for business applications is the test trophy, not the test pyramid. Integration tests are the core layer. For Vaadin applications, two tools cover the E2E layer:

- **Browserless Testing** runs full UI flows, including navigation and validation, without a browser. It gives E2E coverage at near-integration-test speed.
- **Playwright** is reserved for scenarios where actual browser behavior is what you are testing.

TDD still has a role, but inside a spec-first workflow. It fits business logic, services, and APIs better than UI layers.

Coverage should be judged against the specification, not only against code execution. Naming conventions and annotations make this traceability visible and machine-readable. AI can generate and update tests efficiently, but only human review can confirm that they express the intended behavior.

With a solid test suite in place, the next question is what tools support this way of working. Chapter 7 looks at the options, from simple Markdown and Git setups to the AI Unified Process Marketplace.

CHAPTER 7

Tools for Spec-Driven Development

There is a common misconception that spec-driven development requires a special tool, a modeling environment, or a proprietary platform. It does not. A text editor, Git, and an AI agent are enough. The method works because the core artifacts are simple, reviewable, and versioned. No custom format, nothing to install beyond what most developers already have.

That said, tools can make the workflow easier, and the industry has started to catch up. In recent years, several tools have emerged that explicitly put specifications back at the center of development. They share a common insight: AI is more reliable when it works from structured artifacts rather than vague prompts. This is not a new idea, but it is now being built into commercial products and open workflows.

This chapter looks at two of them, Amazon Kiro and GitHub Spec Kit, and explains how they relate to the AI Unified Process. It also introduces the AI Unified Process Marketplace, which is a practical implementation I built to package spec-driven workflows, guidance, and stack-specific capabilities for real projects.

S. Martinelli, *Spec-Driven Development*, Apress Pocket Guides,
https://doi.org/10.1007/979-8-8688-2851-5_7

Tools Are Optional, Discipline Is Not

This holds at any scale. A solo developer can apply the AI Unified Process with nothing more than Markdown files and an AI agent. The specifications provide the discipline. Tools become useful when teams grow, AI usage becomes more frequent, and inconsistency starts to appear. Their job is not to replace the method. Their job is to make the method easier to follow consistently.

A Shift in the Industry

A clear shift is happening in AI-assisted software development. Early tools focused mainly on autocomplete and code generation. Newer tools increasingly move structure, reviewability, and workflow discipline back to the center. Two prominent examples are Amazon Kiro and GitHub Spec Kit.

They differ in style and scope, but they share the same core idea: AI should work from specifications, not invent behavior from loosely phrased prompts.

Amazon Kiro

Amazon Kiro is an AI coding environment that emphasizes spec-driven development and structured guidance for implementation. Specifications and project guidance live in plain Markdown.

A typical Kiro workflow uses three artifacts:

- Requirements.md captures intent and acceptance criteria.
- Design.md documents architectural direction and decisions.
- Tasks.md translates the design into executable steps for the AI agent.

This makes AI interaction more predictable. The agent is not simply asked to build a feature. It follows a defined chain of artifacts.

The AI Unified Process centers on system use cases as executable behavioral contracts. Kiro centers on a requirements → design → tasks workflow. These approaches are compatible, not competing. In practice, system use cases can provide the behavioral precision inside a broader Kiro-style flow.

GitHub Spec Kit

GitHub Spec Kit is not an IDE. It is a toolkit and workflow for structured, spec-driven AI development.

Spec Kit introduces a specify CLI tool, a .specify directory for AI-facing project memory, and slash commands that enforce workflow order. Its life cycle is explicit:

- Constitution
- Specification
- Planning
- Tasks
- Implementation

Each step produces versioned Markdown artifacts. The strength of Spec Kit is workflow enforcement. It reduces prompt chaos and replaces it with predictable AI interactions around named artifacts and ordered steps. That ordering helps teams stay aligned and makes it harder to skip the thinking that should happen before code generation.

Where the AI Unified Process focuses on behavioral precision and traceability, Spec Kit focuses on disciplined orchestration around a defined life cycle.

The AI Unified Process Marketplace

The AI Unified Process Marketplace is the practical implementation I built to support this way of working. It is not a required product. It is an example of how spec-driven workflows, guidance, and stack-specific capabilities can be packaged for real projects.

I built it because existing tools did not package the process and stack guidance in the way I needed for real project work.

The Marketplace is currently packaged for Claude Code, which provides the installation model and slash-command workflow. But the underlying skills are not limited to Claude Code.

A skill is a reusable structured capability that guides an AI agent through a defined task: writing requirements, creating an entity model, drafting a use case, or implementing a use case in a specific stack. The methodology and the skill concepts are portable.

The Marketplace provides

- Core AI Unified Process skills
- Stack-specific skills
- MCP server integrations

It packages AI Unified Process knowledge into reusable, versioned components that can be installed and executed consistently.

The Marketplace repository lives at `https://github.com/AI-Unified-Process/marketplace`.

Core vs. Stack Plugins

A key architectural decision in the Marketplace is the separation between methodology and execution.

Core Plugin

The AI Unified Process Core plugin (`aiup-core`) is stack-agnostic. It provides skills for the core specification artifacts, available in Claude Code as slash commands:

- requirements
- entity-model
- use-case-diagram
- use-case-spec

These operate only on /docs artifacts. The Core understands requirements conventions, system use case structure, traceability rules, ID consistency, and observable behavior enforcement. It does not know anything about frameworks, databases, or UI libraries. This keeps the methodology stable.

Stack Plugins

The examples in this chapter use the aiup-vaadin-jooq plugin. It provides capabilities such as Flyway migration generation, use case implementation, browserless testing, and Playwright testing. In Claude Code, these are invoked as

- flyway-migration
- implement
- browserless-test
- playwright-test

A stack plugin is the extension point that connects the stable process model with a specific technology ecosystem. One team may use Vaadin, Spring Boot, jOOQ, and Flyway. Another may use React, .NET, or a completely different stack. There is no limit to the kinds of stacks that can be added. New stacks can be introduced without changing the AI Unified Process itself.

Skills and Slash Commands

A skill is the reusable unit of process knowledge. In Claude Code, a slash command is simply the invocation form of a skill. For example:

- `/use-case-spec UC-001`
- `/implement UC-001`
- `/browserless-test UC-001`

These are not ad hoc prompts. They are direct invocations of structured skills. In Claude Code, every skill can be invoked as a slash command, so the distinction is mostly conceptual rather than operational. The important point is that the AI is not improvising from scratch. It is following packaged process knowledge.

Because the skills are not bound to Claude Code, the same process knowledge can be adapted to other agent environments.

MCP Integration

The Marketplace can also integrate MCP (Model Context Protocol), an open standard for connecting AI applications to external systems and tools.

MCP becomes useful when an AI agent reaches the implementation step and needs accurate technical knowledge. Without external knowledge, an agent relies on what it learned during training. For widely used frameworks, this is often good enough, but training data has a cutoff date, contains errors, and becomes outdated as APIs change. The result is often plausible-looking code that compiles poorly, uses deprecated methods, or guesses at APIs it does not actually know.

MCP reduces that risk by giving the agent access to authoritative technical knowledge at the moment it needs it. Instead of guessing at a jOOQ DSL pattern for a complex query, the agent can query a jOOQ MCP server. Instead of inventing a browserless testing method, it can ask a Vaadin MCP source for the current API and signatures. In practice, this provides structured access to sources such as Vaadin API documentation, jOOQ DSL references, Vaadin testing patterns, and Playwright automation documentation.

MCP sources can expose many kinds of structured knowledge: framework documentation, DSL references, testing patterns, API schemas, company-internal coding standards, or architecture guidelines. The right mix depends on the project, which is one reason the Marketplace is designed as a layer rather than a closed product.

Specifications define what the code should do. MCP helps the agent do it correctly in the chosen stack. Together they provide both behavioral guidance and technical grounding.

The Marketplace As a Process Layer

Traditional tools try to become the primary place where work happens. The AI Unified Process Marketplace takes a different role. It does not lock you into an IDE, require a specific AI agent, or enforce a proprietary format. Instead, it provides packaged process knowledge that can be used by different agents and in different environments.

You can use it with different AI agents, combine it with Amazon Kiro or GitHub Spec Kit, or use it standalone. It standardizes how AI agents interact with specifications. That is why it is better understood as a process layer rather than as another development tool.

Choosing the Right Tool

Not every project needs the same setup. The right choice depends on team size, the level of AI usage, and how much workflow enforcement you need.

If you are a solo developer or a small team just starting with AI-assisted development, you do not need a dedicated tool at all. Markdown files in a Git repository, a CLAUDE.md or AGENTS.md file, and an AI agent are enough to apply the AI Unified Process. The discipline comes from the specifications, not from tooling.

When a team grows and multiple developers use AI agents in parallel, informal discipline starts to break down. People use different prompt styles, skip steps, and produce specifications of uneven quality. At that point, a tool that enforces workflow order adds real value. GitHub Spec Kit is a good fit here. It is lightweight, CLI-based, and works well for teams that already use GitHub and want more structure without adopting a new IDE.

If your team prefers a full IDE experience and wants AI to work closely with structured artifacts from within the editor, Amazon Kiro is worth evaluating. Its three-artifact structure maps naturally onto AI Unified Process phases, and the IDE integration makes the workflow visible to everyone on the team.

The AI Unified Process Marketplace fills a different role. It does not replace Kiro or Spec Kit. It provides reusable, versioned process knowledge that can be layered on top of any of these tools. Use it when you want consistent AI behavior across projects, stack-specific guidance packaged as skills, or the ability to swap AI agents without rewriting your workflow.

How the Tools Compare

Amazon Kiro, GitHub Spec Kit, and the AI Unified Process Marketplace share the same core insight: AI produces better results when it works from structured artifacts. But they differ in scope, integration style, and what they enforce. Table 7-1 shows a brief comparison.

Table 7-1. *Tool Comparison*

Option	Primary role	Integration style	Workflow enforcement
Plain Markdown + AI agent	Minimal starting point	Any editor or agent	Low, depends on team discipline
Amazon Kiro	IDE-centered structured workflow	Dedicated AI coding environment	High
GitHub Spec Kit	CLI-based life cycle enforcement	CLI and repository workflow	High
AIUP Marketplace	Reusable process layer and stack guidance	Skills, plugins, and MCP integrations	Medium to high

All four options use plain Markdown as the artifact format. This is not a coincidence. Markdown is readable by humans and AI agents, versionable in Git, and requires no proprietary tooling. The differences are in what gets built on top of that foundation.

One thing the table does not capture is adoption cost. Amazon Kiro requires you to change your IDE. GitHub Spec Kit requires you to learn a CLI tool and a new life cycle. The AIUP Marketplace requires you to install plugins and understand the skill model. Plain Markdown requires nothing but discipline. Start with the least you need, and add tooling when you feel the pain that the tool solves.

What to Expect from Future Tools

The tooling landscape around AI-assisted development is moving fast. Amazon Kiro and GitHub Spec Kit were not widely known two years ago. The next generation of tools will likely appear just as quickly, and some of today's tools will change significantly or disappear. Choosing the right tool is therefore less about picking a winner and more about understanding what properties matter.

The first property is open artifact formats. A tool that stores specifications in a proprietary format creates lock-in. If you cannot read your own specifications without running a specific application, you have a problem as soon as that application changes or disappears. Plain Markdown in Git is not just a pragmatic choice. It is a guarantee that your specifications remain readable, versionable, and portable regardless of what tools you use.

The second property is agent independence. A tool that works only with one AI model or one AI provider is a risk. Models improve, providers change pricing, and new agents appear. The AI Unified Process is designed to be agent-independent for this reason. When evaluating new tools, prefer those that treat the AI agent as a replaceable component, not as the product.

The third property is reviewability. Good tooling makes AI behavior more predictable, not less visible. If a tool hides what the AI is doing or makes it harder to inspect generated artifacts, it is moving in the wrong direction. The value of spec-driven development comes from the fact that every important decision passes through a reviewable artifact.

The fourth property is incremental adoption. A tool that requires you to change everything at once will not get adopted. The best tools let you start with one part of the workflow and expand from there. This is true of the AI Unified Process itself: you can start with use case specifications alone, without the full methodology, and still get most of the benefit.

These four properties, open formats, agent independence, reviewability, and incremental adoption, matter more than any short-term feature list. They indicate whether a tool is built for long-term, maintainable, AI-assisted development or only for a good demo.

Key Takeaways

Spec-driven development depends on disciplined specifications, not on tools. The industry is catching up to this idea. Amazon Kiro, GitHub Spec Kit, and the AI Unified Process Marketplace all put structured artifacts, versioning, and workflow order at the center. They differ in scope and style, but they share the same core insight: AI produces better results when it works from specifications.

The Marketplace shows one way to operationalize this in practice. But the underlying idea matters more than the specific implementation. Process knowledge can be packaged, versioned, and reused. That makes AI behavior more consistent across projects, teams, and even across different AI agents.

The next chapter puts everything together with a complete example. A simple task manager walks through every step of the process, from requirements to use case specifications, entity model, implementation, and tests. Small enough to follow in one chapter, complete enough to show how the method works end to end.

CHAPTER 8

Case Study: Building a Simple Task Manager

This chapter is a practical walkthrough of spec-driven development with the AI Unified Process and Claude Code. It uses the Task Manager repository as a small but complete example.

The project is intentionally modest. It is not trying to be the ultimate task manager. It exists to show how specifications, code, and tests can evolve together without drifting apart.

The goal of this chapter is simple: after reading it, you should be able to clone the repository, follow the same sequence, and apply the workflow in your own projects with only minor adjustments.

Project Setup

The project uses a Java stack that is well suited to business applications:

- Spring Boot as the application framework
- Vaadin for the front end
- jOOQ for database access
- PostgreSQL as the database
- Testcontainers for local database setup

S. Martinelli, *Spec-Driven Development*, Apress Pocket Guides,
https://doi.org/10.1007/979-8-8688-2851-5_8

Local Setup

To run this project locally, you need the following:

- Java 25 or later: Any JDK distribution works. Eclipse Temurin is a good default and can be downloaded from `https://adoptium.net/en/temurin`. On Linux and macOS, you can also use `https://sdkman.io` to install and manage Java versions.
- Docker: Download and install Docker from `https://www.docker.com/get-started`. Make sure Docker is running before you start the application. If Docker is not running, Testcontainers cannot start PostgreSQL and the application will fail with a connection error.

Get the Code

Clone the repository and switch to the project folder:

```
git clone https://github.com/ai-unified-process/task-
manager.git
cd task-manager
```

To verify that everything is set up correctly, run:

```
./mvnw spring-boot:test-run
```

This starts the application with the test classpath, launches PostgreSQL through Testcontainers, and opens the application in your browser.

You should see the login screen like in Figure 8-1.

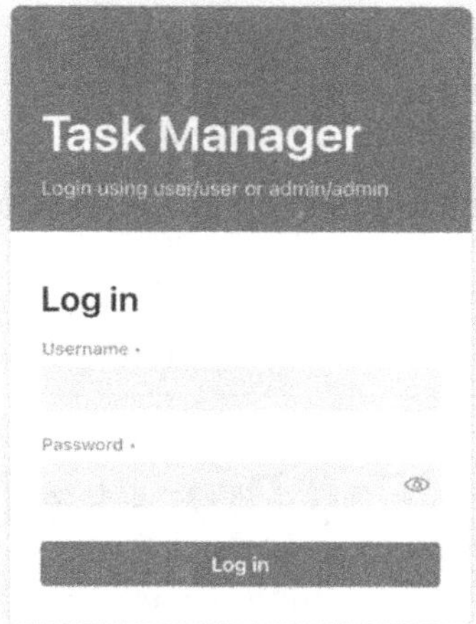

Figure 8-1. *Login Screen*

Steps

The walkthrough is divided into ten steps. Each step corresponds to a Git tag in the repository, so you can inspect the exact state of the project at that point:

```
git checkout <tag>
```

Step	Tag	Description
1	init	Vision and initial project setup
2	requirements	Requirements catalog
3	entity_model	Entity model and glossary
4	use_cases_diagram	Use case overview diagram
5	scaffolding	Project scaffolding
6	database_migration	Database schema migrations

(continued)

Step	Tag	Description
7	spec_UC-006	First use case specification
8	implement_UC-006	Use case implementation
9	test_UC-006	Browserless tests
10	e2e_UC-006	End-to-end tests (Playwright)

Using the AI Unified Process Tools

There is no special tooling needed. A capable AI agent, Markdown files, Git, and clear specifications are enough.

The AI Unified Process adds optional tools and slash commands, documented at `https://unifiedprocess.ai/tools.html`. These tools do not change the workflow. They provide templates, structure, and guardrails that make the workflow easier to repeat.

In this chapter, slash commands are shown as examples. They are there to illustrate a disciplined way of working, not to suggest that the process depends on specific command names.

The Case Study Repository

The repository follows one central rule: the /docs folder holds the authoritative description of system behavior.

The structure looks like this:

```
/docs
├── vision.md
├── requirements.md
├── entity-model.md
└── use-cases
    ├── UC-001-create-task.md
```

```
├── UC-002-view-task-list.md
└── ...
```

Implementation code and tests live under `src/main` and `src/test`.

Step 1: Start with the Vision

The starting point is a short vision in docs/vision.md. It is deliberately small and easy to review. There is no slash command for this step. The vision is written manually, based on what you know about the problem and the users.

For this case study, the system supports only a handful of flows:

- Create a task
- List tasks
- Complete a task
- Handle basic validations and statuses

That is enough to demonstrate the full loop from idea to implementation without turning the example into a large product.

A vision could look like this:

```
# Vision

The **Simple Task Manager** is a collaborative web application
that helps teams manage tasks in a clear and controlled way.

The system focuses on **observable behavior**, **clear rules**,
and **traceability** from requirements to code and tests.
It is used as a case study to demonstrate **Spec-driven Development
with the AI Unified Process**.

The goal of the application is not to be feature-rich, but to
be **well specified**.
```

```
## Business Goals

* Enable teams to create, assign, and complete tasks
* Ensure users see and change only tasks they are allowed to access
* Enforce clear task workflows and business rules
* Keep specifications, implementation, and tests consistent
  over time
```

To view the project after Step 1:

```
git checkout init
```

```
You should see this output:
```

```
Note: switching to 'init'.

You are in 'detached HEAD' state. You can look around, make
experimental changes and commit them, and you can discard any
commits you make in this state without impacting any branches by
switching back to a branch.
```

Step 2: Write the Initial Requirements

The vision is turned into a requirements catalog in `docs/requirements.md`.

The same conventions used throughout the book apply here:

- FR-### for functional requirements
- NFR-### for non-functional requirements
- C-### for constraints

At this point, requirements capture intent, not detailed interaction flow. They define what the system must support so that later use cases can describe how that behavior works.

A small excerpt might look like this:

```
| ID     | Title          | User Story
|--------|----------------|---------------------------------------
----------------------------------------------------------
| FR-001 | Create Task    | As a team member, I want to create
tasks so that I can capture work items for my team.
| FR-002 | Assign Task    | As a team lead, I want to assign tasks
to team members so that work is distributed clearly.
| FR-003 | Complete Task | As a team member, I want to mark tasks
as complete so that progress is visible to the team.
```

This is still lightweight, but it is already versioned, reviewable, and traceable.

Using the AI Unified Process tools, the slash command at this stage is:

```
/requirements
```

This command proposes an initial requirements set based on the vision. The result still needs human review.

To view the result after step 2:

```
git checkout requirements
```

Step 3: Define the Entity Model

With the requirements in place, the next step is the entity model in `docs/entity-model.md`.

To generate the entity model, use this command:

```
/entity_model
```

Even in this small project, the model already includes the concepts needed later in migrations, use cases, and tests:

- Team
- Task
- TeamMembership
- TaskAudit

For example, the Task entity includes attributes such as

- id
- team_id
- title
- description
- status
- assigned_to
- created_by
- created_at
- updated_at

The entity model is more than a database sketch. It is the shared vocabulary of the system. The names defined here are reused in specifications, schema changes, code, and tests.

That matters in the next step, because the database schema should not invent concepts that were never agreed on in the model.

To view the result of Step 3:

```
git checkout entity_model
```

Step 4: Create the Use Case Diagram

Before writing detailed use cases, it helps to create a high-level overview. In the repository, this is a PlantUML diagram in `docs/use_cases.puml`.

The diagram serves two purposes. It gives stakeholders a quick picture of the system scope, and it acts as a checklist for which use cases still need detailed specifications.

The slash command is:

```
/use-case-diagram
```

The output of the command will be similar to the use case diagram in Figure 8-2.

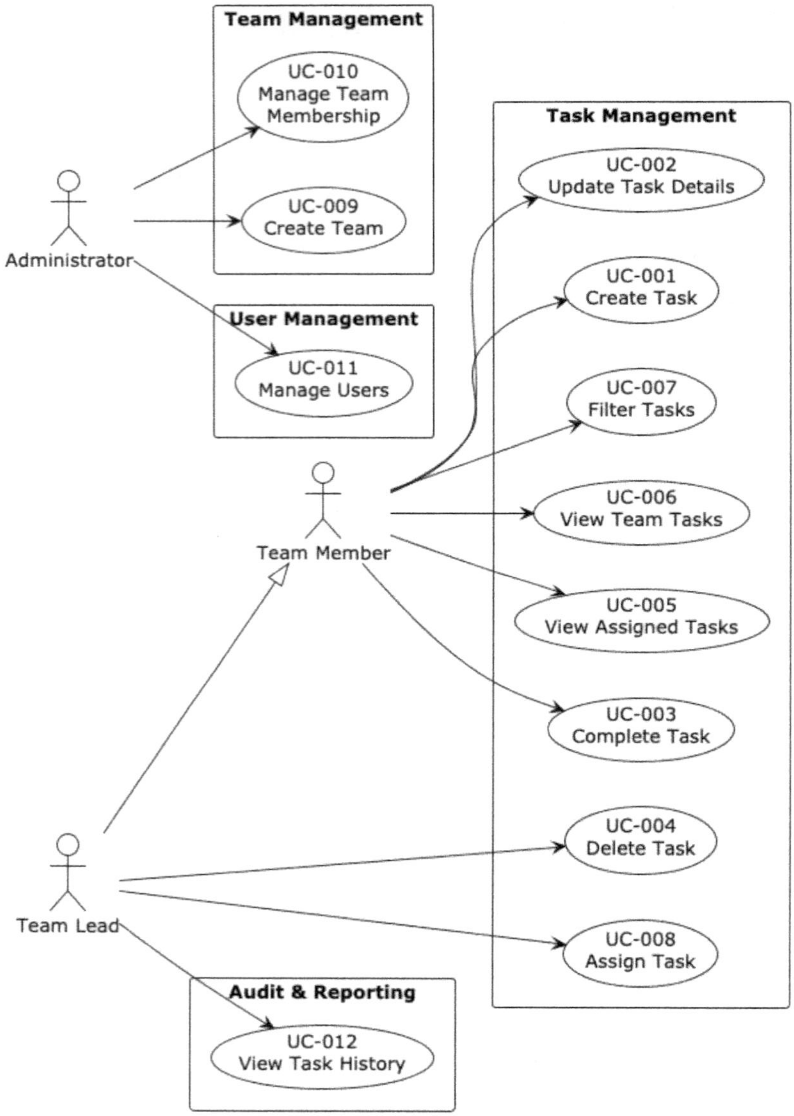

Figure 8-2. *Use Case Diagram*

To view the result of Step 4:

```
git checkout use_cases_diagram
```

Step 5: Scaffold the Project

Once the core specifications are in place, the project needs a technical starting point. This step creates the initial application structure that later gets shaped by migrations, use case specifications, implementation, and tests.

At this point, the specifications already define the direction. The vision explains the purpose. The requirements identify the expected capabilities. The entity model provides the first shared understanding of the domain. The use case diagram shows the main interactions. What is still missing is the application skeleton that gives these artifacts a place to become executable.

The exact way bootstrapping happens depends on the chosen technology stack. In this case study, I use Spring Boot, Vaadin, and jOOQ. That reflects the stack used throughout the example, not a general requirement of spec-driven development. Another team could use a different setup. The workflow would remain the same: specifications still come first.

A basic Spring Boot application can be generated with Spring Initializr. For this example, I start from a template that already includes the basic structure for this type of application, with Vaadin for the UI and jOOQ for database access. This gives the project a working baseline without distracting from the real focus of the chapter.

There is no dedicated slash command for this step in the AI Unified Process Marketplace. That is intentional. Project bootstrapping is strongly stack-dependent and is better handled with the standard generators or templates of the chosen ecosystem.

What matters is that the result is focused, consistent, and ready for the next steps. After bootstrapping, the project should build successfully and provide the technical basis for adding migrations, implementing use cases, and deriving tests. The scaffold is not the outcome of the process. It is only the foundation that allows the real work to begin.

In the repository, you can inspect the result of this step with:

```
git checkout scaffolding
```

This checks out the state of the project after the initial bootstrap. From there, the next step adds the database migration and begins turning the specification into a working system.

Step 6: Database Migration

Before implementing any use case, the database schema must exist. In this step, Flyway migration scripts are created based on the entity model defined in Step 3. Use this command:

```
/flyway-migration
```

The migration scripts create the tables for the core entities: teams, tasks, team memberships, and task audit records. Each script is versioned (`V002__create_team.sql`, `V003__create_team_membership.sql`, and so on) so that the schema evolves in a controlled and repeatable way.

This is a spec-driven step: the migration scripts are derived from the entity model, not invented ad hoc. The attribute names, types, and relationships match what was defined in `docs/entity-model.md`.

A simplified migration excerpt might look like this:

```
create table task
(
    id          bigint        not null primary key
                              default nextval('task_seq'),
    team_id     bigint        not null,
    title       varchar(200)  not null,
    description varchar(2000),
    status      varchar(20)   not null,
    assigned_to username,
```

```
    created_by  username      not null,
    created_at  timestamp     not null,
    updated_at  timestamp     not null,

    constraint fk_task_team foreign key (team_id) references
    team (id),
    constraint fk_task_assigned_to foreign key (assigned_to)
        references "user" (username),
    constraint fk_task_created_by foreign key (created_by)
        references "user" (username),
    constraint ck_task_status
        check (status in ('DRAFT', 'OPEN', 'ASSIGNED', 'DONE'))
);
```

Even this small example shows the connection between model and implementation. The entity names and attributes flow directly into the relational schema.

To view the result of Step 6:

```
git checkout database_migration
```

Step 7: Write the First Use Case Specification

The core of the project is defined in the system use cases located in `docs/use-cases/`.

In the repository, you can already see the naming pattern: `UC-006_View_Team_Tasks.md`, and so on.

Each system use case contains:

- Preconditions
- Main success scenario with numbered steps
- Alternative flows with clear triggers
- Postconditions
- Explicit business rules
- References to linked requirements (FR, NFR, C)

For this walkthrough, we start with UC-006: View Team Tasks. This use case was chosen because it is simple enough to demonstrate the full workflow but rich enough to show filtering, data display, and role-based behavior.

This command is a call of the skill from the marketplace that includes the use case template:

```
/use-case-spec UC-006
```

A compact excerpt could look like this:

```
# Use Case: View Team Tasks

## Overview

**Use Case ID:** UC-006
**Use Case Name:** View Team Tasks
**Primary Actor:** Team Member
**Goal:** View all tasks belonging to a team to understand the
team's workload
**Status:** Documented

## Preconditions
- User is authenticated

## Main Success Scenario
```

```
1. User navigates to the team tasks view.
2. System determines the teams the user belongs to.
3. If the user belongs to exactly one team, the system
   selects it.
4. If the user belongs to multiple teams, the system shows a
   team selector and the user selects a team.
   - If the user has multiple teams, the system selects the
   last used team by default.
5. System retrieves tasks for the selected team.
6. System displays the task list.

## Business Rules

### BR-001: Team Membership Required
Only users who are members of a team can view that
team's tasks.
```

To view the full outcome of Step 7:

```
git checkout spec_UC-006
```

Step 8: Implement the Use Case

At this point, the workflow moves from "Specify" to "Generate."

The use case specification from Step 7 is now turned into working code. The AI agent reads the specification and generates the necessary components: a Vaadin view, service classes, jOOQ queries, and translations.

The key principle is that code is derived from the specification, not invented. The field names, validation rules, and flow steps in the code correspond directly to what was defined in the use case document. If the specification says that the user can filter tasks by status, the generated view will contain a status filter.

For example, the generated UI logic may end up looking roughly like this:

```
statusFilter.addValueChangeListener(event ->
    taskGrid.setItems(taskService.findTasks(teamId, event.
    getValue())));
```

This is where the CLAUDE.md guardrails from the scaffolding step pay off. The AI agent follows the established package structure, naming conventions, and architectural patterns because they are explicitly defined.

To run the skill that implements the use case using Vaadin, Spring Boot, and jOOQ:

```
/implement UC-006
```

To view the result directly:

```
git checkout implement_UC-006
```

Step 9: Write UI Unit Tests

Tests are derived from the same use case specification. Browserless testing allows writing fast, in-memory unit tests for Vaadin views without starting a browser.

The test scenarios map directly to the use case: the main success scenario becomes the happy-path test, and alternative flows become additional test cases. The test verifies that the view behaves as specified, including filtering, data display, and edge cases.

A simplified example:

```
/**
 * UC-006 Main Success Scenario: User with single team Steps 1-3:
 * User navigates to
 * view, system determines teams, auto-selects single team
```

```
 * <p>
 * BR-001: Team Membership Required
 * BR-002: All Team Tasks Visible
 * BR-003: Task List
 * Ordering (sorted by updated_at DESC)
 */
@Test
void user_with_single_team_sees_tasks() {
    // Given: User with access to exactly one team
    login("singleTeamUser", List.of(Role.USER));

    // When: User navigates to the team tasks view
    UI.getCurrent().navigate(TaskView.class);

    // Then: System auto-selects the single team
    ComboBox<Team> teamSelector = _get(ComboBox.class, spec ->
                                                   spec.
withLabel("Team"));
    assertSoftly(softly -> {
       softly.assertThat(teamSelector.getValue()).isNotNull();
       softly.assertThat(teamSelector.getValue().name())
                               .isEqualTo("Development Team");
       // And: Team selector is read-only)
       softly.assertThat(teamSelector.isReadOnly()).isTrue();
    });
    ...
}
```

The important point is that this test exists because the behavior exists in the use case, not because someone later remembered to add it.

To generate the browserless tests:

```
/browserless-test UC-006
```

To view the result:

```
git checkout test_UC-006
```

Step 10: Write End-to-End Tests

In addition to unit tests, end-to-end tests are written using Playwright. These tests run in a real browser against the full application stack, including the database.

End-to-end tests complement the browerless tests by verifying that the complete system works as expected, not just individual components. They catch integration issues that unit tests cannot detect.

A Playwright example:

```
@Test
void user_with_single_team_sees_tasks() {
    // Given: User with access to exactly one team
    login("singleTeamUser", "user");
    page.navigate("http://localhost:" + localServerPort);
    waitForVaadin();

    // Then: System auto-selects the single team
    var teamSelector = page.locator("vaadin-combo-box")
              .filter(new Locator.FilterOptions().
              setHasText("Team"));
    assertThat(teamSelector.isVisible()).isTrue();
    ...
}
```

To generate the Playwright tests:

```
/playwright-test UC-006
```

To view the final result:

```
git checkout e2e_UC-006
```

All three steps, implementation, unit tests, and end-to-end tests, are driven by the same specification. This is the core idea: one spec, multiple derived artifacts.

Iteration: Change the Spec First, Then Sync

Iteration is where the strength of the AI Unified Process becomes most visible. The first ten steps built the system from scratch. But real projects do not end after the first release. Requirements change, users give feedback, and bugs appear. The question is: how do you change a system without losing the alignment between specification, code, and tests?

The answer is simple: change the specification first, then synchronize everything else.

Suppose a stakeholder asks for a change to UC-006: the task list should show a priority column with a defined sort order. In a traditional workflow, a developer might jump straight into the code and update the tests later or never. Over time, this creates drift between documentation and implementation.

With the AI Unified Process, the sequence is always the same:

1. **Update the specification:** Add the priority attribute to the entity model. Update the use case with the new column and a business rule for the sort order. Review the change with the stakeholder while it is still cheap to correct.

2. **Generate a migration if needed:** If the entity model changed, run /flyway-migration to create the schema update. If only a business rule changed, skip this step.

3. **Re-run** `/implement UC-006`**:** The agent reads the updated specification and adjusts the existing code. It does not start from scratch.

4. **Re-run** `/browerless-test UC-006` **and** `/playwright_-est UC-006`**:** New business rules produce new test cases. Existing tests for unchanged behavior stay the same.

Bug fixes follow the same pattern. A bug means the specification is incomplete or the code does not match it. Either way, the first step is to check the spec. If the spec is correct, re-run the implementation command. If the spec is wrong, fix the spec first.

This strict order prevents a common problem: code that works but no one can explain. It also makes AI assistance more effective, because the agent reads the updated specification instead of guessing from vague instructions.

Whether you add a feature, change a rule, or fix a bug, the workflow stays the same. The commands do not change. Only the specification changes. This is the core purpose of the repository: to demonstrate controlled evolution without drift.

Key Takeaways

Chapter 8 walked through all ten steps of spec-driven development on a small but real project. The Task Manager is a learning sandbox, not a production system, but it demonstrates the full AI Unified Process loop from vision to end-to-end tests.

The `/docs` folder is the single source of truth. Vision, requirements, entity model, and system use cases always come before code. When a business rule changes, the specification changes first. Code and tests follow.

System use cases do the heavy lifting. They describe observable behavior in a precise, structured form. They drive implementation, unit tests, and end-to-end tests from the same document. One spec, three derived artifacts.

The result is controlled evolution. Changes stay small, traceable, and aligned with documented intent.

The next chapter explores what happens when systems grow and multiple teams work in parallel: how bounded contexts keep specifications manageable, and how the engineer's role changes when AI handles the mechanical work.

CHAPTER 9

Scaling Spec-Driven Development

Spec-driven development works naturally for individuals and small teams. Specifications are manageable, alignment is straightforward, and conversations happen around a small number of shared artifacts.

The challenge starts when systems grow, multiple teams work in parallel, and AI becomes a permanent collaborator. Scaling requires protecting clarity while complexity increases.

If specifications are the single source of truth, then scaling depends on keeping them small enough to understand. That insight has consequences for architecture, team size, and what software engineers actually do.

Scaling Changes the Bottleneck

In traditional development, scaling usually means adding people. Larger systems require more developers, more developers require more coordination, and coordination introduces meetings, documentation layers, handovers, and integration friction.

Spec-driven development shifts the bottleneck. When AI handles scaffolding, synchronization, and large parts of mechanical implementation, coding speed stops being the primary constraint. What limits progress is clarity of intent. AI can generate code quickly, derive

S. Martinelli, *Spec-Driven Development*, Apress Pocket Guides,
https://doi.org/10.1007/979-8-8688-2851-5_9

tests, and refactor safely. But it cannot clarify ambiguous behavior, resolve conflicting business rules, or design sound architectural boundaries.

When AI speeds up implementation, unclear intent becomes visible much faster. Clear boundaries and precise specifications keep the system under control. Without them, complexity does not grow slowly. It spreads immediately.

Requirements Engineering As the New Bottleneck

If coding is no longer the bottleneck, then something else is. That something is requirements engineering: the work of understanding what a system should do, making that understanding explicit, and keeping it consistent as the system evolves.

This is not a new discipline. Requirements engineering has been studied and practiced for decades. But in traditional projects, its importance was often hidden. When coding took months, nobody noticed that the requirements phase took too long. The slow implementation cycle masked the upstream problem. Developers had time to discover missing rules during implementation, testers found gaps during testing, and the project absorbed the cost through rework and delay.

AI removes that buffer. When implementation takes minutes instead of weeks, every gap in a requirement becomes visible immediately. A vague use case does not produce a mediocre implementation after a long delay. It produces a wrong implementation right now. The feedback loop is shorter, but the consequences of unclear intent arrive faster too.

This shifts the center of gravity. The speed of delivery is no longer limited mainly by coding. It is limited by how quickly a team can make intent explicit and resolve ambiguity. The speed at which a team can deliver correct software is limited by how fast it can produce clear, complete, and consistent specifications. AI cannot do this work. It can suggest use case templates, generate drafts, and check for obvious gaps. But deciding what the system should do, resolving conflicts between stakeholder interests, and choosing between competing business rules requires human judgment and domain knowledge.

At scale, the challenge intensifies. If you work with multiple bounded contexts, each one requires its own requirements engineering. Stakeholders may interact with several contexts. A business rule in Order Management may contradict an assumption in Billing. A change in Customer Portal may affect how both other contexts expose data. Someone has to detect and resolve these cross-cutting concerns. That work does not disappear when contexts are well separated. It becomes more structured but not less important.

This changes how software engineers operate. Understanding stakeholder needs cannot be a one-time phase at the start. It has to continue throughout the project, because every new use case and every change depend on that shared understanding. Engineers need direct access to domain experts. Regular refinement sessions are not optional but essential. The quality of these conversations determines the quality of the specifications, and the quality of the specifications determines everything downstream.

It also means that the skills teams need are shifting. In the AI era, the most valuable team member is not the fastest coder but the person who can sit with a stakeholder, ask the right questions, spot contradictions, and turn a vague business need into a precise system use case. This skill mattered in the pre-AI era as well, but in the AI era, it is critical for success.

Team Size in the AI Era

One consequence of AI-assisted development that rarely gets discussed: the optimal team size goes down.

In many traditional projects, large teams exist not just to build features but to compensate for missing clarity. Developers interpret requirements differently. Testers rediscover business rules by accident. Architects reconstruct intent from code. Integration teams resolve conflicts between modules that were never properly separated. Most of this work is coordination overhead caused by ambiguity.

When behavior is anchored in explicit system use cases, when requirements are versioned, and when AI synchronizes code and tests from these artifacts, much of that ambiguity-driven effort disappears. Smaller teams can handle larger systems.

AI does not replace software engineers. But fewer software engineers are needed when intent is already clear. Alignment lives in the specification core instead of being reconstructed through communication loops. Of course, reduced team size only works when the architecture supports it. That is where bounded contexts come in.

Bounded Contexts As the Structural Scaling Mechanism

Specifications scale only when they remain bounded. Human cognition has limits. AI context windows have limits. A monolithic system with hundreds of use cases and hundreds of entities overwhelms everyone.

Bounded contexts, a concept from Domain-Driven Design by Eric Evans, solve this structurally. A bounded context defines a clearly delimited business capability with its own requirements catalog, entity model, system use cases, version history, and architectural responsibility.

In a Self-Contained System architecture[^1], each bounded context owns its UI, logic, and data. It evolves independently. Its specification core stays manageable. Specifications remain reviewable, AI prompts remain focused, merge conflicts decrease, and cognitive load drops.

Compare this to one massive repository with hundreds of interdependent artifacts. With bounded contexts, you have multiple smaller systems instead, each with a coherent scope. You add new bounded capabilities rather than enlarging a single monolith.

This does not mean contexts are isolated. They interact through events, APIs, and shared identifiers. But these integration points are explicit contracts, not hidden dependencies. For a human or an AI agent, this means you can work inside one context and only need to understand the contracts it has with its neighbors, not their internals.

This is the scaling limit many organizations overlook. When systems grow, they often respond with more layers, more coordination, and more process. But the real limit is simpler: people and AI can only work well when the scope stays understandable. When a specification cannot be understood on its own, it is too large or too entangled. Keeping each artifact small and focused enough to remain understandable, reviewable, and executable matters more than any process improvement.

Bounded Ownership and Team Responsibilities

When each bounded context owns its full specification core, responsibilities shrink to a manageable size. A team does not own parts of a monolith. It owns a business capability.

Within that boundary, the team takes full responsibility for the entire life cycle: defining and refining requirements, maintaining the entity model as the shared language of the domain, writing and reviewing system use cases that describe observable behavior, synchronizing the implementation when use cases evolve, and protecting the architectural boundaries of the context.

There is no separate specification team, coding team, and testing team. The specification is owned, not handed over. This cuts handovers, translation loss, and coordination overhead. Instead of ten people touching the same specification set, a few engineers fully own one bounded context. Parallel development follows naturally because specification cores do not overlap.

Smaller teams are not just a side effect of AI. They follow naturally from bounded ownership. When a team owns one coherent business capability, it does not need to be large.

What Engineers Actually Do

When systems are well bounded and AI handles more mechanical work, the classic split between analyst, developer, and tester becomes less useful. Inside a bounded context, members share responsibility for the entire behavioral life cycle rather than passing artifacts from one role to the next.

Engineers spend more time clarifying observable behavior with stakeholders and making sure that what is written actually reflects business intent. System use cases are developed together with domain experts, which makes rules explicit and uncovers edge cases early. Engineers also put more effort into refining use cases, spotting missing or ambiguous rules, reviewing AI-generated diffs, and checking architectural consistency.

Less effort goes toward repetitive scaffolding, boilerplate, and low-level refactoring. AI handles that translation from specification to implementation.

In practice, the daily questions shift: Is this use case complete enough to implement? Does this AI-generated diff match what we actually specified? Is this new feature pulling behavior across a boundary it should not cross? These are judgment calls that require domain knowledge.

The focus shifts toward specification integrity and clear ownership. Fewer handovers are needed, and responsibilities come back together inside the team.

Parallel Development Without Coordination Explosion

Bounded contexts enable structural parallelism. Team A evolves Order Management. Team B evolves Billing. Team C evolves Customer Portal. Each team updates its own specification core, reviews behavior locally, synchronizes code through AI, and deploys independently. Cross-system integration happens through explicit contracts like APIs or events. Hidden database coupling disappears.

Because specification cores are separated, teams rarely collide. AI benefits directly from this separation too: an agent operating in one bounded context does not need to ingest the entire enterprise repository. Context stays manageable and synchronization gets more accurate.

Architecture and AI scalability reinforce each other.

Governance: Lightweight but Strict

Scaling does not require heavier processes or elaborate governance structures. It requires discipline. As systems and teams grow, clarity does not disappear because there are too few rules. It disappears because the essential rules are not applied consistently.

In a spec-driven environment, a small number of principles is enough:

- Behavior never changes without updating the corresponding specification first.
- Stable identifiers are durable references and are never reused.
- System use cases describe observable behavior only, not hidden implementation details.
- Each bounded context owns its own specification core.

These principles are made explicit in versioned guideline files and treated with the same seriousness as source code. When they change, the change is reviewed. When they are violated, it is visible. Governance stays lightweight but is never informal.

Consistency comes from applying a small set of clear rules without exceptions, not from more meetings or more documentation.

Flow Over Sprints: Why Kanban Fits Better

Sprint cadence can be useful when teams need a regular rhythm for planning, alignment, and feedback. But in a spec-driven environment, the natural unit of progress is not the sprint. It is the use case. In traditional development, the two-week rhythm compensates for unclear intent.

In a spec-driven environment, that problem is solved differently. Use cases are explicit and reviewable before implementation starts. AI synchronizes code and tests from them. The feedback loop is built into the specification process itself, not into an artificial cadence. When intent is already explicit and reviewable, a fixed sprint boundary often adds less value. In that situation, continuous flow tends to fit the work better.

Kanban fits better. The natural unit of work is a single use case. It moves through a defined sequence: Draft, Review, Approved, Implemented, Verified, Deployed. That is continuous flow, not a batch. A Kanban board models this directly, and work moves forward as soon as it is ready, not when the next sprint starts.

This also matches how bounded contexts deploy. Each bounded context owns its pipeline and specification core. It can release independently at any point. Sprint-gated releases work against this. A use case that is fully verified should not wait two weeks for a sprint boundary.

The spec dashboard described in the next section supports this. It gives visibility into use case status, coverage, and regression stability at any time. You do not need a sprint review to know what is done and what is drifting. The dashboard shows it continuously.

The one practice worth keeping from Scrum is regular stakeholder collaboration for refining use cases. But that does not require sprints. A short weekly or biweekly refinement session works just as well, without the ceremony.

DevOps and the Specification Pipeline

DevOps supports this flow directly. A CI pipeline that runs on every commit does more than check compilation. In a spec-driven project, it verifies that behavior still matches the specification: unit tests cover the business rules of each use case, E2E tests confirm the observable flows, and the regression suite ensures that previously verified use cases have not broken. When a test fails, the pipeline identifies not just a broken build but a specific use case whose behavior has drifted from what was specified.

Because each bounded context has its own pipeline, deployment does not require coordination across teams. Teams deploy when their use cases are verified. In this model, the pipeline checks whether the implemented behavior still matches the specified behavior on every change.

Progress Tracking and the Spec Dashboard

Traditional progress tracking counts closed tickets, burns story points, and measures velocity. These signals can show activity, but they say little about whether the system is actually aligned, consistent, and protected against regressions.

In a spec-driven environment, code is not the primary artifact. Specifications are. Progress needs to be measured at the level of behavior, not activity.

A functional requirement is not complete because someone closed a ticket. It is complete when its intent is expressed in a reviewed system use case, when that use case is implemented, and when derived tests verify the defined behavior. The central question shifts from "Did we finish the task?" to "Is the intended behavior specified, implemented, and verified?"

Because the AI Unified Process enforces stable identifiers and explicit traceability between requirements, system use cases, code, and tests, alignment becomes observable. Teams can measure how many requirements are structurally integrated, how many use cases are fully verified, and whether any part of the specification core is drifting from implementation.

Instead of velocity dashboards, teams can maintain a lightweight spec dashboard directly in Markdown inside the repository, as shown in Table 9-1.

Table 9-1. *High-Level Progress*

Category	Total	Complete	In progress	Not started	Coverage
Functional requirements	12	8	2	2	67%
System use cases	10	7	2	1	70%
Use cases with full test coverage	10	6	3	1	60%
Regression stability	—	100%	—	—	Stable

Coverage here is derived from structural completeness, not lines of code. A requirement is complete when it is linked to an approved system use case that is implemented and fully verified. A use case is complete when it is approved, synchronized with code, and protected by passing tests that cover its main and alternative flows.

The regression stability row deserves clarification. Regression means unintended breakage of previously implemented behavior. When a new use case is added or an existing one changes, the regression suite checks that earlier use cases still work as specified. If all automated tests pass, regression stability is strong. If previously passing tests start failing, the system has regressed.

For deeper visibility, alignment can be tracked per use case, as shown in Table 9-2.

Table 9-2. *Use Case Tracking*

Use case	Linked FR	UC status	Code	Unit	E2E	Regression	Integrity
UC-001	FR-001	Approved	✔	✔	✔	✔	Strong
UC-002	FR-002	Approved	✔	✔	✔	✔	Strong
UC-003	FR-003	Review	✔	×	×	✔	Partial
UC-004	FR-004	Draft	×	×	×	—	Weak

Code means implementation exists and is synchronized with the specification. Unit means business logic is verified. E2E means behavior works across the full system. Regression means adding or changing this use case did not break previously verified behavior.

In an AI-accelerated environment, generating code is cheap. AI can produce thousands of lines in minutes. But alignment is not automatic. Without discipline, faster generation increases the chance of hidden inconsistency. Progress in a spec-driven system is measured by how precisely intent, behavior, implementation, and verification fit together, not by how much code exists.

Key Takeaways

When AI makes implementation faster, the limiting factor is no longer coding speed. It is the ability to define behavior clearly enough that humans and AI can work from the same understanding. Explicit specifications, stable boundaries, and disciplined ownership matter more than ever.

Bounded contexts are what make scaling manageable. They keep specification cores small enough to understand for humans and AI alike, reduce coordination overhead, and let smaller teams fully own a business capability. You scale by adding new bounded capabilities, not by enlarging one shared specification core.

As AI takes over more mechanical work, engineers spend less time translating intent into boilerplate and more time clarifying behavior, reviewing changes, and protecting boundaries.

Scaling spec-driven development does not require heavy governance. A small set of rules applied consistently is enough: change behavior in the specification first, keep system use cases focused on observable behavior, preserve stable identifiers, and let each bounded context own its specification core.

CHAPTER 10

Best Practices, Pitfalls, and the Road Ahead

A few years ago, I started building a volunteer management system using AI tools. The code came together fast. After a few weeks I had something that looked like a working application. But I could not always explain why it worked the way it did, what assumptions had been made, or whether the behavior really matched the intent.

Speed without intent is not productivity. It is just faster confusion.

Spec-driven development is my answer to that problem. Not more process, not heavier documentation, but one simple discipline: make the intent explicit and stable before any code is generated. In the AI era, that matters even more, because the team and every AI agent need the same point of reference.

This final chapter brings together what I have learned from working this way. It covers what makes the discipline effective, where teams tend to lose it, how to introduce it without turning it into a burden, and where the approach reaches its limits.

Discipline over Complexity

The method itself is not complicated. Write the specification. Derive code and tests from it. When behavior must change, update the specification first and let everything else follow.

S. Martinelli, *Spec-Driven Development*, Apress Pocket Guides,
https://doi.org/10.1007/979-8-8688-2851-5_10

The difficulty is staying consistent under pressure.

A developer fixes a bug directly in the code and does not update the system use case. A business rule changes in a meeting but never makes it back into the specification. A requirement ID gets reused because it seems convenient. None of these mistakes looks dramatic in isolation. Together they create drift.

The structural rule that prevents this is simple: every behavior change starts in the specification, without exception. Drift does not begin with a large failure but with one small exception that nobody notices.

Where the Discipline Pays Off the Most

Not every system needs the same level of rigor. A short-lived prototype or a throwaway script does not need structured use cases. The overhead is not justified.

The picture changes as soon as a system is expected to live and evolve for years. Long-running business applications do not become hard to maintain because of size alone. They become hard because they accumulate hidden decisions, undocumented rules, and local fixes that nobody fully understands anymore.

System use cases address this. When observable behavior is written down explicitly, with preconditions, main flow, alternatives, and postconditions, a new developer or reviewer can understand what the system is supposed to do without reverse-engineering that intent from code.

AI strengthens this argument rather than weakening it. AI reduces the cost of writing code dramatically, but it does not reduce the cost of misunderstood intent. If a specification is vague or inconsistent, AI will simply produce vague or inconsistent results more quickly.

How Spec-Driven Development Fails in Practice

It rarely fails loudly. Table 10-1 shows how it usually happens.

Table 10-1. *Failure Modes*

Failure mode	How it starts	How to fix it
Vagueness	Words like "normally," "should,"or "as needed" appear in specs. AI picks one interpretation. Developers pick another.	Replace vague language with explicit rules. Define measurable outcomes and observable postconditions.
Over-specification	Use cases drift into describing database schemas, UI layout, or internal structure. They become brittle when architecture changes.	Keep specs focused on observable behavior only. If it cannot be verified from outside the system, it does not belong in the spec.
Weakened traceability	Requirement IDs are reused or ignored. Links between intent, behavior, and code are broken.	Treat stable identifiers as structural connectors, not labels. Never reuse an ID. Reference them consistently across all artifacts.
AI bypassing specs	A developer asks the agent to "improve this" without referencing a use case. Code-first thinking returns through the back door.	AI commands must always reference a specific Use Case ID. Synchronization must be intentional and diff-based.
Frozen specifications	Code changes without corresponding updates in use cases. The specification loses authority and becomes outdated documentation.	Specifications are living contracts. If behavior changes, the use case is updated first. Always.

Review Cannot Be Automated Away

Automation makes execution faster. It does not make the intent correct.

A specification still has to be reviewed for clarity, completeness, and domain accuracy. Generated code still has to be checked against the behavioral contract. Tests still have to verify what the specification actually says, not what the developer or agent assumed it meant.

Tests protect observable behavior as the system evolves. They prevent prevent and catch regressions early in the development process. They give the team confidence when changing code. But a test can only check what it was written to check. If the specification is incomplete or wrong, a perfectly generated test suite can still reinforce the wrong behavior.

Human review remains necessary for one reason: only a person can decide whether the intended behavior is actually right for the business. AI can detect inconsistencies between artifacts. It can derive likely test cases. It can point out missing conditions. But it cannot take responsibility for domain correctness.

Spec-driven development does not reduce human responsibility. It moves that responsibility to where it is the cheapest: at the level of intent, before misunderstandings reach code, tests, and production.

Scaling Without Losing Coherence

When AI handles more of the scaffolding, synchronization, and repetitive implementation work, coding capacity stops being the main bottleneck. Lack of clarity becomes the bottleneck.

Clarity does not scale without limits. Human attention is finite. AI context windows are finite. Once a specification core grows too large to read and review comfortably, review quality and understandability both start to collapse.

Bounded contexts are the practical solution. Each bounded context owns its own Requirements Catalog, its own Entity Model, and its own system use cases. The specification stays small enough to review and stable enough to govern.

Scaling then means adding new bounded capabilities, each with its own clear specification and ownership, rather than extending one specification core until nobody can fully understand it. Architectural boundaries are therefore not only a design concern. They are a precondition for maintaining clarity.

Introducing the Practice

Adopting spec-driven development is not only a technical change. It changes where people focus their attention and what they do first.

Developers who open the IDE before anything else will feel slower at the start. Writing a system use case before writing code is unfamiliar, especially under delivery pressure. Stakeholders who are used to informal requirements may also see it as extra work.

These reactions are predictable. They do not mean the approach is wrong. They mean people need to see it work before they trust it.

The fastest way to build that trust is to start with a part of the system where behavior is already contested or unclear. One hour spent clarifying a use case, compared to several days spent fixing a misunderstanding later, makes the value visible very quickly.

Keep the first use cases small. One clear main flow, a handful of alternatives, explicit postconditions. Review it as a team, not in isolation. Specifications become useful only when the whole team relies on them.

The goal at the start is not a perfect specification. It is the habit of writing intent down before implementation begins.

Maturity Develops Gradually

Teams rarely move from code-first development to a fully spec-driven way of working in one step. That is neither realistic nor necessary.

The first stage is often writing specifications after implementation. That already helps, because at least some intent becomes explicit. But the real shift happens when the specification comes first and implementation follows it.

Over time the workflow becomes more natural. New behavior starts with an updated System Use Case. Tests are derived from it. AI works from structured artifacts instead of vague prompts. At that point, the team is no longer depending on discipline in isolated moments. The workflow itself reinforces the discipline.

Maturity is not measured by the number of documents a team produces. It is measured by whether intent and implementation remain aligned. A team with a small set of well-maintained use cases is in a better position than a team with extensive documentation nobody trusts.

When Not to Apply Full Discipline

A short-lived prototype, a quick experiment, a script that will be thrown away: the overhead of structured specifications is not justified. Speed of exploration matters more than long-term clarity.

The deciding question is simple: will this system be maintained, extended, or handed over to others? If yes, making intent explicit early reduces cost later. If the system is genuinely temporary, a lighter approach is enough.

The method is pragmatic, not dogmatic. Apply enough discipline where the future cost of ambiguity will matter. Apply less where it will not.

The Road Ahead

The cost of producing code keeps falling. AI can already generate scaffolding, tests, boilerplate, and many kinds of implementation work in seconds. As these capabilities improve, the value of manually writing code line by line will continue to decline.

That does not make specifications less important. It makes them more important. They are the control surface for AI-assisted development. Instead of asking an agent to build something from a vague description, a team can give it a stable behavioral contract and review the result against that contract.

Better tooling will come. Tools that validate specifications, detect inconsistencies between artifacts, enforce traceability, and flag underspecified behavior are a natural next step. But these tools will only help teams that already understand the underlying discipline. Tools can reinforce clarity. They cannot replace it.

Where to Start

Take one piece of behavior in a system you know well. It does not need to be large or complex. Choose something with a clear actor, a clear goal, and at least one rule that has caused confusion or argument before.

Write a system use case for it. Define the preconditions. Write the main success scenario step by step. Add at least one alternative flow. State what must be true when it completes. Keep it short enough that another person can review it without fatigue.

Then review it with one other person who did not write it.

That review is where the value becomes visible. Assumptions surface. Terms that seemed obvious turn out to need definition. A rule that everyone thought was agreed on turns out to have two different interpretations.

Once the use case is reviewed and agreed upon, implement it. Reference the Use Case ID in the code and tests. When the behavior changes later, update the use case first.

One use case is enough to start. The value of the second one is easier to see once you have seen the first.

Final Reflection

The central problem in modern software development is not that we cannot produce code fast enough. It is that we often do not make intent clear enough before we start producing it.

Spec-driven development addresses that problem directly. It makes behavior explicit before automation begins. It replaces implicit assumptions with shared, reviewable contracts. It anchors change in versioned artifacts that both humans and AI can follow.

The experiment that opened this book gave me code quickly. What it did not give me was confidence. I could see the result, but I could not always explain it, verify it, or extend it safely. The AI Unified Process grew out of that experience. It is my attempt to put clarity back at the center of software development, exactly where AI makes it most necessary.

Protect bounded contexts. Protect stable identifiers. Protect observable behavior. Clarity is not a nice extra. It is the constraint that determines whether software can evolve sustainably.

www.ingramcontent.com/pod-product-compliance
Lightning Source LLC
Chambersburg PA
CBHW060348040926
51002CB00020B/349
* 9 7 9 8 8 6 8 8 2 8 5 0 8 *